YOU SHOULD LEAVE NOW

Going on Retreat to Find Your Way Back to Yourself

BRIE DOYLE

FOREWORD BY CHRISTIANE NORTHRUP

BROADLEAF BOOKS
MINNEAPOLIS

YOU SHOULD LEAVE NOW
Going on Retreat to Find Your Way Back to Yourself

Copyright 2021 Brie Doyle. Printed by Broadleaf Books, an imprint of 1517 Media. All rights reserved. Except for brief quotations in critical articles or reviews, no part of this book may be reproduced in any manner without prior written permission from the publisher. Email copyright@1517.media or write to Permissions, Broadleaf Books, PO Box 1209, Minneapolis, MN 55440-1209.

Cover design: Juicebox

Print ISBN: 978-1-5064-6695-8
eBook ISBN: 978-1-5064-6696-5

To my mom, who taught me the value of creativity, individuality, and spirituality. To my dad, who taught me grit, self-discipline, and to always question the status quo.

CONTENTS

CONTENTS

Part III: The Inner Trajectory of Retreat

Part IV: Transitioning Back Home

FOREWORD

When I read *You Should Leave Now*, I was struck by the fact that I needed its message as much as any woman. I need to take Brie's advice and leave now. I'm on the brink of a new retreat-filled life. I can feel it. And it is long overdue.

Do you know what I'm good at? Work! Writing books, giving lectures on women's health, doing conference calls, helping friends and family with health issues. I have just finished revising the fifth edition of *The Wisdom of Menopause*. Last year I fully updated and revised the fifth edition of *Women's Bodies, Women's Wisdom*—what I call the post-#MeToo version. Both were huge projects. I have discipline to burn.

After years (or maybe lifetimes) of walking around with the yoke of duty, obligation, and self-sacrifice on my shoulders, discipline is a pattern that has established itself in my bone marrow. I was born in the Year of the Ox. I haven't taken a break for longer than one week in fifteen years. As an obstetrician/gynecologist, it served me well through many years of staying up all night, delivering babies, and performing surgery while also trying to figure out how to take care of my children and my relationships. It was the unspoken rule of surgical training that the person who could stay up the longest and work the hardest was the winner—the MVP of medicine, a true warrior. (Conventional medicine is rife with war metaphors.) And what type of warrior goes on retreat or takes a rest? Doctors are trained to be "in the foxhole"—to be at war with our bodies, with germs, and with disease and sickness and to be the tireless champions of people who will die unless we are hypervigilant.

But not so fast. The truth is, there wouldn't be nearly so much disease and suffering if we all learned how to retreat and practiced it regularly. To do this, we have to be shame- and guiltproof. We need to have enough self-love and self-acceptance inside to stand up for ourselves and our worth. And that is exactly what *You Should Leave Now* teaches us. It's an owner's manual for self-love, self-esteem, and the actual step-by-step plans for tapping into the courage it takes to surrender to our innate need for rest, reflection, and restoration.

Writer and sociologist Brené Brown has stated that guilt means "I made a mistake," whereas shame means "I am a mistake." Women have had centuries of enculturation into our "less than," shameful status. As the late Anne Wilson Schaef put it, "The original sin of being born female is not redeemable by works." As a result of this unconscious programming, we live in fear of being called selfish. To avoid that awful emotion of shame, we overgive.

In her book *The Art of Extreme Self-Care*, my colleague Cheryl Richardson wrote a chapter called "Let Me Disappoint You." It speaks volumes to the fact that no woman is able to care for herself adequately without being a disappointment to someone else who wants her attention, her resources, or her time—even if that someone is the well-practiced inner critic inside her own head who just can't seem to get it all done. Trust me, the world we have all been brought up in runs on the unpaid and unacknowledged labor of women and those who operate out of the feminine caring principle.

But there's another way that is now emerging as a new generation of women realizes that we cannot continue this unsustainable overwork and underrest any more than our Mother Earth can continue to be exploited for endless productivity and profit. Here's my prescription for you and for myself:

1. Read *You Should Leave Now: Going on Retreat to Find Your Way Back to Yourself.*
2. Put a retreat time in your calendar. Maybe start with a long weekend, then—as you read through this book—allow the

details of the retreat to flesh themselves out in that powerful gift we're all born with: our imagination.
3. Repeat regularly. (I recommend every six months.)

Here's what will happen: We are going to find ourselves restored.
And like a field that has undergone the miracle of regenerative
agriculture, we will bloom with health and happiness like never
before.

—Christiane Northrup, MD, *New York Times* bestselling author
of *Women's Bodies, Women's Wisdom*; *The Wisdom
of Menopause*; and *Goddesses Never Age*

PREFACE

Dear One,

It is with humility and excitement that I welcome you to this book and to your personal retreating journey. If you have found me and this book, then you are seeking even more power in your life. You are ready for your own next level. If you have come to this book, perhaps you've tried many different self-care tactics and are looking for something even more profound to assist you in bringing your greatest gifts to the world.

It is my belief that retreating is the alchemy you've been seeking and the way to reconnect you with your center and most powerful source of light.

In over two decades of working with people young and old, studying human behavior, and watching true transformation unfold, I know that retreating has the power to radically change lives.

You are no exception. Retreating will change your life too.

We all come to retreating for different reasons. Some of us stumble upon our retreat seemingly blindly—maybe we follow a friend or we serendipitously end up in the right place at the right time. Some of us are simply seeking a new experience. Some may use retreating as a tool for personal healing. Under the right circumstances, our retreats can inspire profound insights, help us find our true voice, increase our creativity, and connect us to our own divinity.

No matter what brings you to retreat, let me assure you that taking time away to do one is always the right decision. You cannot know now what benefits, breakthroughs, personal understandings, or synchronicities await you. But by the end of your retreat, you will.

My deepest wish is that this book will remind you that no matter your need—fun, healing, inspiration, and so on—you always have retreating in your toolbox of self-care tactics to bring you back to yourself. You need no fancy talismans, sites, or teachers, only yourself and a quiet space.

May this book be of benefit to you and yours.

Your inside self awaits.

With love,
Brie

Part I

REASON TO LEAVE

Chapter 1

BOUNCING OFF
THE BOTTOM

The wound is the place where the light enters you.
—Jalal al-Din Muhammad Rumi, *The Essential Rumi*

I am at home with my third child, a boy, who we named Quinton Jack after my father. He is just over a year old. He toddles around the living room with his blocks and trucks as I stare out the window across the street to where we are building our dream home. My two other children are at preschool.

I can see larger, real-life versions of the same trucks my son plays with demolishing our old house to turn it into something beautiful. The sun glimmers through the window of the rental house where we now stay.

It is quiet with only baby babbles and the hum of the dishwasher, and I know I am lucky to live this life. I haven't always lived this way—I was a teacher, and my husband an entrepreneur—but I do realize how privileged we are now. I also know that when your insides are not well, it doesn't matter what your life looks like on the outside.

And something inside me is not well. I do not feel happy like I believe I should be. I am regularly grateful, yes, but also darkly, penetratingly unhappy.

Not many people know this. In fact, no one does. I have mastered the art of being polished, putting forth the right look and feel despite what bubbles beneath. It is not because I am fake, this practiced exterior. It is because I am strong. I take on everything no matter the consequences for myself. I am used to being the one whom other people depend on. Falling apart is not an option.

So I keep quiet.

But inside, my secret weighs a million tons. It leaks out the seams in arguments with my husband, aloofness with my children, and disassociation with myself. I don't know who I am anymore, and I can't seem to remember what lights me up. I am hungry to connect to a deeper purpose beyond daily duties and obligations. I don't know what I want and why I feel so low.

What I do know is that I have been better.

What I am sure of is that I used to be a light. I used to be fun and sexy and sharp and highly motivated. I used to dance through life, one adventure after another, enjoying every last drop.

Now I am just treading water. I look back and forth from shore to shore, unsure of which direction to go, emotionally exhausted and lacking my typical pep to get me to the other side.

I live in one of the healthiest communities in the United States, so says *Outside* magazine. This is both a blessing and a curse. I see people going on jogs and catching their second yoga class for the day, and it makes me want to barf. I do it too, but with robotic-like enthusiasm. Not because it fills me like running on the trail or skiing or lifting weights used to. I do it because this is what health looks like in my community. Maybe if I fake it long enough, I will feel it too.

No one tells you how desperate you can feel as a new mother and how foreign you can feel to yourself, how alone. I have close friends and family all around me, but I am not used to or comfortable with being the one who people need to be "there for." I am the caretaker and have always taken pride in being able to pick my own self up no matter the blow.

It is in these months that for the first time in my life, I find myself looking for some sort of description for what is wrong with me. Am I depressed? Anxious? Hormonally imbalanced? Is it stress? Lack of sleep? Am I eating the wrong food?

I want an answer for this incessant hollow feeling.

Something.

Yet I yearn to take responsibility for my own life. Though I have hit a low, I know on some intuitive level that my body, mind, and spirit are trying to communicate something to me.

Though I want a simple answer and quick solution, I am a gritter and a grinder. I was raised by middle-class, hardworking parents. I know the value of digging in because I've watched my dad wake up in the wee hours of the morning and catch a bus to earn a living for our family my entire life.

I've seen my mom raise three kids and run a household with the help of not a single person—always saving pennies, offering us experiences instead of things, and giving every ounce of her time and energy to all our needs. Working hard has been modeled for me my entire life.

I believe that pain, even the darkest kind, carries messages for us, if only we can sift through and find them. Hidden in our pain are whispers of the spirit, beckoning us to find courage to make a change. But it feels impossible to find the lessons when you can't manage to see a doorway out of your own agony.

Yet in my heart, I keep believing that if I do the hard work and don't run to seek a quick solution, maybe a sign will come, and my discomfort will lead me somewhere.

And finally, it does.

"I think I need to go on a retreat," I say to my husband one night at dinner amid squeals and gurgles and splats, the sounds of young children at the table.

He stays quiet.

I watch his eyes and await his response. I realize that me leaving now—with all three kids under six years old, a construction project underway, and him regularly traveling for work—is no small proposition. I understand how hard it would be to keep this ship afloat if I step out of the picture now.

But I also know that my husband sees me. Despite how we have changed in the twenty years since we started dating, he knows me to my core, the best me. He can tell how dimly my light flickers now. I know he can see it.

"Yeah," he says without much hesitation, "you should absolutely do it."

That very night, with fear in my head and a nervous elation in my heart, we sit down together to book a weeklong retreat for just me in Costa Rica.

Travel has always filled me, and solitary retreats have always reconstructed me. I've taken meditation retreats by myself since I was in my teens. When I was a young girl, it was my mom who told me about Catholic nuns, living in solitude to further develop their inner lives. Something about this always called to me; it made sense to me on a fundamental level.

And at twenty, when living abroad in Nepal, I studied under a Tibetan Buddhist meditation master. I spent years learning from him and had kept up a practice of retreating at least once per year.

But having three children has made the leaving feel more difficult. At this point, it's been three years since I've been on a retreat.

I know that if I remember the power behind this practice I have done for years to strengthen my inside self, I can find my own sense of redemption not only for myself but for my beautiful family that deserves a more available version of me.

The time for me to leave comes, and it feels like a ripping at the seams. With my youngest son only fifteen months old, I fear I've made the wrong decision. *What if one of my kids gets sick and I'm not there to take care of them? What if an emergency comes up and I can't make it back in time?* My head spins wildly out of control with "what-ifs." I find myself seeking reasons to back out in the weeks leading up to my departure.

Thankfully, I don't.

o o o

I arrive at the retreat center by myself. I am not a part of any program or group. I want to be alone. Talk to no one. Explain nothing. I want space, time to rest, time to reflect and read.

And so I do. Day by day, under the Costa Rican sunshine, I grow stronger. The entire first two days I sleep. Through everything. Meals, classes, all of it. I show up to not one yoga or meditation class offered on-site. And as a person who always shows up for things, it feels pretty good to not show up for a damn thing.

By my third day, I feel physically strong again. Now it is time to dig into my mental and emotional self. I read Gary Zukav,

Caroline Myss, and Eckhart Tolle alone for hours in my bungalow. I journal on my porch or by the pool as I watch everyone else at the center scurry to classes and connect with each other. I dance naked in front of the mirror by myself to Beyoncé. I feel beautiful and at home in my own skin again.

After a few days of rebuilding myself alone, I feel the pull for connection once more. I still don't want to join an organized group, but I want to talk to people, at least a little bit. At dinner one night, I meet three women, successful professionals who become little angels for me this trip. They see me swinging solo and invite me to sit with them to share a meal.

They ask me questions about being a mother, and I pick their brains about what it feels like to run a construction company of six thousand men, or to be the only female lawyer at a big-time firm, or to be going back to school for a second PhD.

These women are powerhouses. And the funny thing is, as I fantasized about what it must feel like to live their lives, they'd been dreaming about what it must be like to live mine. We all sought retreat from the unmanageable pace of our lives back home. These women are a piece of my rebuilding, mirrors and reminders that though our outside lives may look very different, our inside lives are so strikingly similar.

My new friends leave the center before I do. I am on my own again, as I intended. I sit on the beach on the last night as the sun goes down, finally feeling full again—like myself, a new self. I am ready to go home and press play on the life I'd been living in pause. But only because I stepped away to rediscover myself again.

The challenges I'd faced back home were not situational; they were bigger than that. They were problems of the spirit. Before I left, I no longer belonged to myself. I had outsourced all of my energy, given every last drop of myself to the needs of everyone else, as women so often do. So it is in retreating that I reclaim how to care for and connect to myself in a new and updated way.

I don't presume that you come to this book in the state of internal despair I was in. Or maybe you do. Either way, you've come to the right place. It is my honor and my life's work to encourage you to take a retreat at least once per year for yourself.

This book will walk you through the whys and the hows. There are messages waiting for you that will only be found if you choose to leave. And despite what you might think now, you as well as *all* those around you will benefit from your sojourn.

I can't wait to take this journey with you.

Chapter 2

THIS
MODERN LIFE

For it is not physical solitude that actually separates one from other men, not physical isolation, but spiritual isolation. It is not the desert island nor the stony wilderness that cuts you from the people you love. It is the wilderness in the mind, the desert wastes in the heart through which one wanders lost and a stranger. When one is a stranger to oneself then one is estranged from others too. If one is out of touch with oneself, then one cannot touch others.

—Anne Morrow Lindbergh, *Gift from the Sea*

I gaze out the window at the breathtaking Himalaya mountains as the Druk Airbus makes its way into Paro International Airport in Bhutan, South Asia. I am giddy and can hardly believe I've made it this far. Exhaustion hangs off me, as I'm still recovering from traveling from the United States to Thailand just a few days ago. And now from Thailand to Bhutan. Nevertheless, I am elated to be here by myself.

This is my first real retreat since becoming a mom. My one-year-old daughter is with my husband at home, which feels a million miles away. I will be gone for a total of three weeks, my stay in Bhutan a small portion of my trip. I haven't left my daughter for more than a few hours before now. So this trip is a huge jump for me.

But it also feels like an essential one. I could have gone for retreat closer to home. I could have retreated somewhere in Colorado, or maybe even California or Arizona. I didn't have to travel this far.

But I am seeking a feeling, a connection, an adventure, and an intimacy with myself that I found here in Asia nearly ten years before as a younger woman studying abroad in Nepal.

I remember getting lost in the Pilgrims Book House in Kathmandu for hours. The smell of the old binding on the books, the incense and the taste of the chiya tea as I sat surrounded by prayer flags in their outdoor courtyard are still etched into my memory. It was a little sanctuary with the most obscure books hidden amid Kathmandu's crowded streets. I spent every spare moment reading about Eastern philosophy, yoga, meditation, Ayurvedic healing, plant medicine, and more.

Never had I felt so alive and inspired. Never had I felt more aligned with who I really was and what I wanted to learn.

The focus on the inner world is what draws me back to Asia now.

I wasn't sure I wanted to have children. I was a freedom-seeking, independent type of gal. I feared that I'd lose all my liberties if I had kids. I worried I'd never travel alone again and I'd have to sacrifice every bit of who I was to be a mother.

My husband and I made a pact when I was pregnant with my first child that once per year, each of us would take retreat. Even when we had kids. And even when they were still young. We believed it was as much for them as it was for us—to take care of them, we had to be healthy ourselves. No matter who objected or what society posited about being a parent, we'd go.

I feel immense gratitude for my husband and my choice to come as the plane lands in Bhutan, a country that measures gross national happiness (GNH) as opposed to GDP as an alternative indicator of progress and development.

I miss my family incredibly, but just being here feels right on a gut level. I get off the plane and inhale the fresh, mountain air. I grab my small backpack filled with only things that I need—no diapers, baby snacks, or toys—and walk through the airport on clouds.

I find my driver waiting for me on the other side of customs, and I am delighted to learn that he speaks Nepalese, like I do. Instead of English, we laugh at each other as we attempt to exchange what Nepali language we both know.

Not twenty minutes into the country and I already feel like myself again. An old self and a new self, both. A self that I've been waiting to meet again.

o o o

We live in decadent times.

With the click of a button, we can get anything we want by tomorrow. We can connect to anyone in the world within seconds. We can eat yesterday's freshly caught bluefin tuna from Japan today and book a flight this morning that will get us to Dubai by tonight. Our children grow up with instant answers to their questions thanks to Google, and we don't even have to go outside to check the weather to determine what we'll wear today.

But considering all we've gained, have we lost something too?

The capacity of what we can do in the world right now is extraordinary. These advancements are real and powerful but also have energetic and spiritual consequences that we don't regularly consider.

With this kind of innovation comes a new pace, vibration, and way of being in the world. In an instant, old values are thrown out, and new ones stand innocently untested in their place. And we jump in, unaware of how we, down to our very core, will be affected until after the fact.

Our human needs are ever the same—certainty, variety, love and connection, significance, growth, and contribution.[1] And so we take our needs and push them onto this new paradigm to see how they'll fit and uncover how we'll manage.

Seeking love and connection, with a side of variety, we sit lovingly close to our partners on the couch—and simultaneously scan our social media feeds for two and a half hours a day (up almost an hour per day since 2012)[2] while watching TV after a long workday. And this is how we satisfy our need for connection.

Desiring of purpose, and unsure of how to meet our need for significance, we turn to the seduction of acquiring things. This way, at least on the exterior, it appears we have all we need to those viewing our daily play-by-plays.

We order another pair of jeans or search for a new car, a second home, or book another trip and tell ourselves we'll worry about the financing later. With hungry ghost-like insatiability, we buy more, and more, and more.

With the average American holding four credit cards $10,000 deep in debt on each one,[3] we have developed an ugly, secret habit to attempt to fill our void for significance.

And because spending this kind of money is normal, and we yearn to contribute, we work even longer hours to be able to afford this extravagant lifestyle we've built. Eighty-six percent of men and 67 percent of women in America work well beyond forty hours per week.[4]

We pursue the human need for growth within the confines of our workplace, whether we're happy or not, because where else could we possibly experience growth when we spend every waking moment at the office or plugged in, reachable and checking email and social media accounts?

Our bare feet rarely touch the earth, our skin doesn't see the sun, we don't sleep enough, we hardly know where our food comes from, and we raise generations of children who model our sedentary behavior, who'd rather play *Fortnite* than hide-and-seek. And we assess our value by how many followers we have and likes we get.

It's no wonder one in eight young adults in America experiences depression and reports difficulty focusing.[5] With this trajectory, it's not entirely shocking that suicide is the third leading cause of death among fifteen- to nineteen-year-olds.[6] We're just so dang busy, distracted, and personally disconnected.

Our poor children are the innocent bystanders of a culture left unchecked. Their anguish is the same as our own, wildly waving red flags, showing signs and symptoms of spiritual distress, younger and younger these days. Their collective angst is a sign that something is not right in the way we live our lives. They are our canaries, going into coal mines, many never to come out again, in hopes that we'll see them, help them, offer guidance.

If the declining mental well-being of our children is not a message that something needs to change on a societal level, I don't know what is. Unwell children on a grand and increasing scale are litmus tests of our culture as a whole. Mental and emotional health challenges permeate every corner of society. And after months of isolation from each other and overuse of technology because of COVID-19, things aren't looking any better in this realm.

With our basic need for certainty now in question, our very sanity at risk, we are swept away by life's tumultuous waves, desperately clawing our way back to the surface for our own air.

It's no wonder so many of us struggle to feel good at our core. It's not surprising we feel so depleted. When we live arrhythmic lives, undervaluing what the natural world intended for our species—disregarding the critical elements of sleep, movement, rest, and nourishment—our organism cannot thrive. We have no access to deep energy. We feel hollow and beat down, tired and uninspired.

This portrait of American life may or may not be an accurate depiction of your own life. But surely, we all see pieces of ourselves in here. The point is, it is not entirely our fault. We are all victims of a pace, normalized behaviors, and a society, all of which we cannot entirely control.

The sad truth is, much of what is considered ordinary in our culture today is toxic and unsustainable on a spiritual and energetic level. Our society values progress more than wellness, *doing* over *being*. But living this way has consequences, as declining mental health statistics continue to show us.

Yet despite the waves you bump up against now, you do have some control. And it starts on a personal level. You cannot change what is outside before you change what is inside. Whether you're already familiar with your sense of center and ground or you are caught amid life's swirls seeking land, retreating is how you find your way back to the shores of yourself.

But retreating is not currently a normalized, societal practice. Going against that which isn't practiced by the masses takes courage. Nevertheless, you must leave what is comfortable and safe because you know what might have worked before no longer holds true today, right now.

For yourself, your family, and your community, you must prioritize your own mental and emotional well-being. Even when others around you don't understand or your children are small or your work life is robust. Especially then. You must retreat to remind yourself of your own truth and inner fire.

When you feel an urge or discomfort at your core, know that this is enough of a reason to step away for retreat. When you know there is more for you—you can be more, do more—it is time to step away and go inward.

So trust that which is bigger than yourself. Honor your discomfort, or your inspiration, as a message to seek space within yourself. Acknowledge the call to your own hero or heroine's journey, understanding that you cannot know what awaits; you can only trust what sparked that initial fire to go.

Because you know that if you stay put, something in you dies. That toxic track takes hold and rots you from the inside out until your wake-up call is so significant it takes years for you to heal.

But you have a way now, a window, an opening. It is simple but not easy. For a weekend, a week, or maybe a month per year, let your spirit hibernate. Go against the shoulds, the needs, the desires, and the expectations. Retreat to stabilize the soul against all odds.

You must do it alone, for this is a solitary journey. This is not a slaying of dragons but a slithering out of old skin. A rebirth with brand-new wings awaits. No one else can do this kind of work for you. Growing is a solo mission, and if you want to contribute anything of value to your precious self, family, community, and world, then you must do the work, at first, yourself.

So Dear One, there is only one question left. Have you heard the call?

Chapter 3

THE FEMALE PREDICAMENT

> Over time I've come to see what society calls being a "good woman" or a "good doctor" or a "good mother" came dangerously close to an invitation for me to lose myself in serving others at my own expense. I've learned that I am able to provide optimal service and friendship to others only to the degree that I'm also tuning in to what I need to do for me.
>
> —Christiane Northrup, MD, *Women's Bodies, Women's Wisdom: Creating Physical and Emotional Health and Healing*

I am ten years old, and if I am sure of anything, it is that I will be the first girl to play baseball in the major leagues. I love baseball more than I love anything. I have more cards than both of my brothers combined. I flip through baseball beckets for hours every day. And because my dad says the world is harder on a girl than it is on a boy, I practice my swings and ground balls more than any boy in my neighborhood.

It is the first day of a new season, and I am on the Orioles. We have orange jerseys, and orange is my favorite color. It's going to be a good season. My dad is the coach, and my younger brother is on the team too. I am the only girl on our team.

We sit in a pack on the first day of practice with our gloves, our new hats, and mouths full of Big League Chew. My dad calls me up to the front of the group. He puts his hands on my shoulders and turns me around to face the boys.

"This," he says, "is a girl." The group starts laughing, and I can't help but giggle too. "We don't treat her any differently than we do each other. She is a part of our team. She's just as good as any of you. Just wait, you'll see." The boys in my group nod in agreement with my dad, the coach.

Their acknowledgment makes me feel like I can do anything and like they see me. I can't think of another time in my entire ten-year-old life when I've been prouder to be a girl.

O O O

The role of the woman in today's society is complex and rapidly shifting. We are at times weighed down by standards of the past, yet we have choices and liberties our mothers and grandmothers never had.

We can have lofty careers and children too. We can skip the kids and travel the world. We can marry or never consider it, divorce five times, date both genders, disidentify from gender, and on and on and on.

It is beautiful and, at times, personally disorienting. For though these choices bring freedom, they also carry with them a divisive new narrative that at first feels empowering (*I can do it all!*) and second is deeply troubling (*I should do it all and am not doing enough*).

The inner conflict this creates for women leaves us feeling hollow and powerless. It's as if no matter how much we do, in any one category, it is never quite right or enough. The private spiritual turmoil of women today is real and pulsates at the core of every one of us.

Both a blessing and a curse is that we are biologically and socially conditioned to find our value in what we do for others. So we compensate for this limitless void by doing more in every arena of our lives. As a result, we are exhausted and personally and spiritually disenfranchised.

One truth remains: no matter our choices, one of our greatest assets is that we give. It is near social code that a woman must give of herself. Be it to our families, careers, causes, social circles, friends, or foes, we give. For us, this giving creates pride and a sense of both meaning and place in our pack.

Building community is an intrinsic historical and biological need among women. Author and speaker Alison Armstrong speaks about our feminine ancestors—the gatherers, often smaller in stature and weaker in physique to men due to less testosterone—and how they found power among hordes of other gatherers. Male and female partnerships in cavewoman times weren't near as egalitarian as they are today. Women were possessions and prey to predators seeking to spread their seed and raise their offspring.

In order to fend off unwanted hunter-like attention, to stay protected from other threats to safety, and to provide for their clans, women drew from their established community of other gatherers.[1]

This holds true even today. There is great benefit to investing time and effort in our community. Who will bring us dinner after surgery or the birth of a new baby? Who can our children grow up with, play sports with, have sleepovers with? Who will be there after a devastating loss? Who will offer a shoulder when we learn of a partner's infidelity? Who knows to the very core what it means to be a gatherer? The other gatherers in our community.

Connection to community is not just important; it's physiologically hardwired. And every woman knows, in order to build our communities, there must be shared trust among gatherers. And to do this, we must give—time, energy, resources—to prove our value and trustworthiness. Break this trust, and you find yourself alone in a metaphorical wide-open field locking eyes with a hungry tiger licking his lips.

There is a selfless quality required to build a sturdy community. You must remain nonthreatening and team minded. Cavewomen lived together, raised their young together, and foraged together when the hunters were out doing their work.[2]

These days, we still look to our community for social and emotional support, but often we do the rest alone. We want friends, but we raise our children, cook the food, tend the house, earn the money, and more on our own. This puts even more pressure on the women of today. Not to mention, many of us are now hunters, too, providing for our families on top of it all.

We must give to our children, our partners, our careers, and our communities in order to stay afloat in the world today. Somewhere at the very bottom of that list, after we've given to all those around us, is the notion that we give to ourselves too. But not too much as to appear selfish.

Despite deep social conditioning, physiological wiring, and personal expectations, I believe our collective consciousness is ready for a change. When we live only to please the group, something inside us is lost and wasted. We are in desperate need of a shift in thinking.

Many of us are beginning to wake up and see that this archaic model of everyone else before the self is not only unsustainable but detrimental. Not merely on a personal level but on a societal one. And not just to women and girls but to all of humanity.

A woman loves nothing more than to be and feel full. Full of life, full of love, full of inspiration, full with a child, full of passion to share with others. With giving as our greatest gift, when we are full—like the mother's breast, swollen with milk—we give from a place of unendingly replenishable reservoirs.

But without proper nourishment, our magic balm dries up.

We must first fill ourselves.

We must first fill ourselves.

We must first fill ourselves.

It bears repeating because though it may be easy to believe, it is just so hard to practice.

Women have always been the great steerers of spirit and spreaders of consciousness. With our communities behind us, the reach of our influence and true social networks expands far beyond what can be seen on a social media screen.

Marketers know that when it comes to the household, decision-making power lies with the woman. According to Consumer Reports, up to 80 percent of purchasing choices for the home today are made by a woman. And not only that; we take care of so many people beyond just ourselves—aging parents, children, friends—we have the multiplier effect.[3]

The reach of our influence is significant. This holds true not just for the purchasing of goods but for ideologies, habits, trends, spirituality, psychology, and more. When one woman models how to take care of herself, a community chain reaction begins. Especially if her happiness permeates her very existence for all to see.

Other women notice, take stock, and seek the same for themselves. They talk about it, share with their friends, and think about it. They ask questions, learn more, and try it out for themselves and their families.

If each woman was to model filling herself before she filled others as a new paradigm, just think what that would do for generations of girls and all kids in general! Think of what it would do for relationships, where each individual feels full and encourages the other to do the same.

Think of what it would do for our psyches, which for so long have been trained to serve all else first. Imagine how it would feel to know that deep in our core was a message that proclaimed loudly, "*You first, your turn, you have so much more to share when you take care of yourself. You deserve this and are worth it.*" Just imagine the confidence, lightness, inspiration, and connection we'd feel.

Retreats root us in our strong connection to spirit. Our children yearn for us to create new feminine archetypes to live by. It is time to model for all of society how when we take care of ourselves first, all around us benefit. Woman as martyr worked for cavewomen and cavemen. But our world calls for something greater on a global level: for an elevation of consciousness for all.

In these rapidly shifting times, we need the gentle yet firm grip of a woman's inner compass to steer our ship forward and gently usher in the much-needed change. Building upon our ancestors who had no choice but to do everything for others, it is time now to evolve. Retreating is the first step in your journey back toward the self for the good of all around you.

Chapter 4

RETREAT, YOUR STYLE

When you receive spiritual instruction from the hands of another, you do not take it uncritically, but you burn it, you hammer it, you beat it until the bright, dignified color of gold appears.
—Chögyam Trungpa Rinpoche,
Cutting Through Spiritual Materialism

I am in the closet when my mom comes to pick me up from the weekend retreat with my church. It is dark, and I am alone, and this is not what I thought this weekend would look like.

I am thirteen, obstinate, and adult-like in my mind but still clinging on to my youth—on both the inside and the outside. Though with each new zit and crush, it is rapidly disappearing.

I am the firstborn in my family. A rule follower. A pleaser. A girl. I am not yet old enough to question authority, aside from my parents. And it just so happens that my best friend in my confirmation group is a boy named Matt. Matt is also on our weekend retreat in Estes Park, Colorado.

I don't *like* him, like him. It's not like that. He just reminds me of my brothers, and he likes rap and baseball too. So we are friends. He recently shaved "Public Enemy" into his fresh buzz cut. Watching him be an altar boy in our church each Sunday with this kind of marking and roll his eyes up there makes me laugh. It makes me feel powerful. Like he can do the dirty work, and I can just watch and enjoy the benefits of his rebellion.

So we are friends.

Sister Margaret sat us all down at the beginning of the weekend and gave us the list of a million rules for the retreat. Among them is *Girls and boys are not to go in each other's rooms*. She is clear with predictable nun-like gruff, and I already know I am not planning to push any limits.

I can't speak for Matt though.

We enjoy a nice group hike in the mountains and hear the adults talk about how they found God in their lives. I listen distantly and in no way self-reflectively. I am not yet sure about God. But so far, I'm having fun here.

After dinner in the mess hall, we are to go back to our rooms and shower, grab our journals, and meet for a nighttime reflection session. I say goodbye to Matt after dinner and do my duties.

On the way to the group session, I walk by Matt's room so we can walk to the community hall together. I knock on his door, and he answers. "Just a sec," he says, "I have to grab my journal." He leaves the door open, and I wait in the hallway.

We are a tad late (his fault, not mine), and he throws things around his room searching for his journal. I can see him from the hallway, and it makes me giggle. Mid laugh, I feel a firm grip around my wrist and hear a punishingly familiar voice.

"Excuse me, Ms. Doyle. What part of the rules did you not understand?!" It is Sister Margaret. She is bloodred in the face, and her eyes are bulging. Mine are now too. My wrist hurts from where she is grabbing me.

"I didn't go in! It's not what you think! I didn't do anything wr—"

"Enough!" she says. Matt comes running to the doorway (still without his journal). "I've seen what I need to see here. Matthew, you come with me too." She leads me by the wrist down the hall away from the community space. Matt is yelling and kicking the wall, telling her we didn't do anything wrong and it's not my fault.

But not me. I am quiet and embarrassed and ashamed. I didn't do anything wrong. I didn't even put a foot in his room. But I do not protest.

Sister Margaret puts us both in closets far away from each other so we can apologize to God for what we've done until our parents can come and pick us up. As far away as Matt is, I can hear him yelling and now cussing from the closet. It makes me laugh and feel powerful. He's so ridiculous. I doodle in my journal in the dark, both afraid and not.

These rules feel so silly to me. *I didn't do anything wrong*, I think to myself again in the dark.

If this is how we're supposed to find God, I think I'll have to keep looking.

O O O

We all have the opportunity in this lifetime to be clairvoyant crystals of truth for ourselves and others. But sometimes we get so mired by the swirl of duties, distractions, expectations, and mindless habit patterns that we lose our luster.

Retreating is how we again find our own clear light.

The word *retreat* is defined as "the act of moving back or withdrawing." It is most often used in terms of combat or spirituality. "To pull back from that which is dangerous, difficult or threatening," says Webster's Dictionary.[1] The different conditions for use feel so dissimilar, but are they really?

We live such full lives. We have people to love, many things to keep us occupied, material possessions, and endless personal and professional aspirations. We are completely immersed in these beautiful lives we've created, as we should be.

And the routines we construct sustain us. Adults and children alike benefit from having predictable patterns in our daily lives. Yet if we do not pull out of our carefully crafted schedules from time to time, these very habits and calendars begin to run our lives as opposed to the other way around.

In practice, a retreat is literally leaving for a chosen period of time to seek respite for inner development. Most often, retreats are done away from your normal surroundings, as new settings stimulate growth. A practitioner can leave for a night, a weekend, a week, a month, or even longer.

In the past, retreats have been associated with religious devotees. However, with the pace of life today, we're all beginning to see the benefit of pulling away to foster sanity in our lives.

But retreats not only support mental health; they inspire creativity. One of the earliest paradigms for the creative process was crafted by British writer Graham Wallas. Wallas suggested that the creative process consists of four components:[2]

- preparation
- incubation
- illumination
- verification

"Preparation" is seen as the "input mode," like a computer—constantly receiving data or ideas. "Incubation" is the "processing mode." This is a time when the input cooks. Here you forget about your inputs and just let them be—this is the phase of relaxation.

"Illumination" is the "output mode" that comes as a result of incubation. Often, flashes of insight come during the incubation period, and illumination is where these insights are shared.

Finally, there is "verification." In verification, the illumination is compared to reason and possibly even received by a larger audience. It is here that creative insights are weighed for validity and inspiration.[3]

Of the four stages—preparation, incubation, illumination, and verification—can you guess which one is most frequently missing in our lives today? You guessed it: incubation.

Susan Cain, author of the groundbreaking book *Quiet: The Power of Introverts in a World That Can't Stop Talking*, says about the workplace that "today's emphasis on group work is so lopsided that there's little time for solitude."[4] I believe this phenomenon permeates all facets of our lives, not just work.

If incubation is anything, it's a solo act, without distractions. If there's little time or value placed on the importance of incubation, this would imply that we're not bringing near the creative insights and breakthroughs to the illumination and verification stages that we're capable of.

We can do and be more.

Creative insights come from experiencing each of the four stages. What sets great minds apart from the common person is the ability to access this creativity with regularity and reach verification with creative outputs. This is impossible without making space for incubation.

We hear these sentiments echoed in the writings of great scientists, artists, and inventors. Wolfgang Amadeus Mozart wrote in a letter to his friend in the late eighteenth century, "Provided I am not disturbed, my subject [creative idea] enlarges itself, becomes methodized and defined and the whole, though it be long, stands almost complete and finished in my mind, so that I can survey it, like a fine picture or a beautiful statue, at a glance."[5]

Rudyard Kipling agreed the key to gaining access to this inner wisdom was "not to think consciously" but to "drift."[6] Daily life doesn't allow for this kind of constructive escapism or "drifting."

Whether we seek to express ourselves as a mother, an artist, a doctor, a volunteer, or a daughter, we all yearn for creative inspiration. We must be disciplined and hold space for our solitude amid a world that values being constantly plugged in and together.

Retreats are best experienced on your own, even if you are a part of an organized program. They can take place among a group— a community is nice—but true personal growth is solitary.

A retreat is different from a family vacation, a girl's weekend, or a reunion with friends. Though each is restorative in separate ways, woven throughout a retreat is a higher spiritual purpose, a deeper intention of self-awakening. It need not have any particular religious affiliation, though it can. Religious practices are not a necessary part of a retreat.

Retreating allows us to see our lives with different lenses so we understand what shifts need to be made to our daily lives back home. This brief spaciousness allows us to live with a greater sense of inner alignment and intention.

Perhaps by stepping away, you uncover that you want to start a morning wellness routine, love your partner more outwardly, make more time to play with your children, show appreciation to a coworker, or even break away from a toxic relationship. It is often only in pulling away from your day-to-day that you can see these dire needs in your life with clarity and gain the courage to act on them upon your return. This is the creative insight we're all yearning for.

Deeper still, retreating allows you to see your true nature. You cannot always hear yourself in a crowd of others, even if those others are your girlfriends, your family members, or closest intimate partners.

Old patterns of girlhood run deep. We want to be included, invited, and a part of the community. So from a very early age, we learn to be pleasing and likable.

As young girls, we are taught that pleasing others is one of the most important ways to feel significant. Do as teachers say; always include everyone; don't be too loud, too emotional, too needy, too sexy, too smart, too dark, too masculine, too anything. Stay predictable. Do what is expected. Don't stray outside the lines.

As a result, it is not immediately that we appreciate the value of doing something alone and finding our own way. It feels counterintuitive and even dull compared to the frenzied lives we live back home. But this is the exact shift we need to hear our own voice again.

I remember a retreat I went on in my twenties at a Buddhist monastery in Colorado. I arrived at the monastery in the late afternoon. We were to be in silence for the week. This delighted me. This retreat center suggested four meditation sessions per day, with a group prayer service in the late morning.

The truth was, I didn't want to go to the prayer ceremony. I had retreated here numerous times in the past and always participated in the prayer ceremony. But this time, intense resistance percolated in me. I felt like that young girl again waiting outside of Matt's room, not entirely sold on the "rules" of the center, yet feeling like I needed to follow protocol so as not to cause an issue.

The ceremonies here were always in Tibetan, and though beautiful, the practices felt esoteric to me. My inside self pulled hard to skip it this time. I wanted to get outside and hike in the incredible snow-capped mountains when I wasn't meditating instead of being inside all day. I spent too much of my time at home working and not enough wandering outside. That was what I really needed, and I knew it.

Yet my old patterns crept back in more quickly than I would have liked to admit. As I woke on the first morning of my retreat, I found myself stumbling to the prayer room for the collective ceremony against my better judgment.

Almost unconsciously, I showed up daily to be accepted, follow protocol, and gain likability among the monks and other monastery inhabitants (who weren't even talking to me and who surely didn't care).

Of course, there is nothing wrong with following protocol and wanting to be liked. Group prayer services can be lovely and powerful. But after days of trying, they still lacked meaning for me.

When I finally found the courage to stop going on day five, I couldn't help but wonder, How much of myself have I given away for the sake of what other people think of me? Where else do I do this in my life back home? And most importantly, what do I owe myself now? Certainly at least as much as I give to others.

It felt good to be rebellious and miss morning prayer. Not because I wanted to disappoint people, but because it felt like I was finally listening to that voice I stepped away to hear. I found my core again. And I actually listened this time. It is so easy to fall out of practice doing so.

"Be Bad" became my own internal motto, not in a reckless way but in a way in which I really examined what was expected of me. Not just on retreat, but in the outside world too. I could bring something in, try it on for size, and give my *Bad* self permission to say no if it didn't feel right on a gut level. I still use my "Be Bad" monitor whenever something starts to feel off in my core.

It was from this resistance that I began to ask myself the question, What truly serves me on retreat? Does it look different from what is expected on a typical retreat? Does it change every time? Are there common themes or practices that always bring about shifts? Are there ones that never do that I can let go of? Are there ones that don't feel great but I know I need to be disciplined about and stay with anyway?

It is with this same sense of flexibility that I hold space for my participants on every one of the retreats that I host. I always leave space for participants to create their own element(s) along with my suggested list. Because after all, retreating is about your individual evolution.

There is no teacher, tightly crafted schedule, or set of ideals that will work for any one person all the time. If personal growth is what you're after, then you have to be unflinchingly honest and present with yourself about what works and what doesn't. And you have to be open to adapting at any given moment.

Considering this and holding space for fluidity, here are the Elements I use, practice, and introduce as supportive on my retreats. Take a look, try them on, and see what your gut tells you. We'll go over them in detail later in the book.

Elements of Retreat

1. Solitude
2. Disconnect from home and work life
3. Reconnect to basic needs
4. Expansive self-study (mental and emotional)
5. Healthy introspective practices (physical)
6. Meditation
7. Silence and other ascetic practices
8. Resistance as teacher
9. Connection to the divine

The beauty of these Elements is that they can each be reached in your own particular way. We'll dig deep into the meaning of each of them in part 2. But just know that by using these nine Elements of Retreat, you can create or be a part of any retreat and have an incredible personal awakening on your time alone. Furthermore, they're open-ended enough that anyone, no matter your belief system and background, can apply them for incredible personal results.

Be bad, and go get 'em!

Chapter 5

GET YOUR MIND RIGHT

[The] mind is the master weaver, both of the inner garment of character and the outer garment of circumstance.

—James Allen, *As a Man Thinketh*

I am sixteen and driving to my friend Lacy's house after track practice. Lacy has her parents' red-hot convertible with leather seats. We feel like superstars as we drive through town singing Lauryn Hill at the top of our lungs.

School starts in a week, but we have two-a-day track practices in the summer to get us prepped for the season. We are in between sessions, and we head to Lacy's house to grab some food before we start our late afternoon practice.

Lacy is a beauty. She's tall and leggy with thick chestnut locks that she normally wears long. She just chopped her hair this morning before practice for a change, and I love her hip, new look. She now rocks a cute, stylish bob. It's currently pinned up and in pigtails to keep it out of her face during practice.

We round the corner to her parents' house, and I can already taste the turkey and cheese sandwich with pickles that I plan to devour once we get there. The same one we had at my house yesterday.

We are growing and athletic girls, ravenous at every moment we are not practicing. She haphazardly parks her parents' car in the driveway, and we run inside to eat as if *this* was the actual race.

When we enter, her mom is standing at the top of the staircase, in between us and the kitchen. I smile politely and say hello.

"Hi, Mom!" Lacy offers as she throws her bag on the floor and keys on the living room table.

Her mom grips the banister with a look of disgust on her face. She is not looking at me; she stares at Lacy. "My God, Lacy. What did you do to your hair?" Lacy, a social and typically confident gal, a beast on the track field, shrinks instantly.

Her mom's eyes are wild, and I can see her puffing up her chest, gaining power and confidence in the same moment her daughter drains of it. She chortles slightly and shakes her head.

"I dunno what you were thinking! What boy would ever date you now?" She raises her voice as she says it, then looks at Lacy fiercely. She huffs off to another part of the house. A few tears fill Lacy's eyes. But she does not let herself cry. Stunned, I wait in the entryway as Lacy runs up the stairs to grab a few snacks for us.

Visions of large and delicious sandwiches leave my head. I now feel sick to my stomach. My mom would never say something like that to me, no matter how hideous I looked. I wonder if something happened to her mom to make her so unkind. I gaze around the living room at the perfectly positioned furniture and blankets and out to the beautifully manicured garden. Lacy's mom's behavior so starkly contrasts these surroundings and it shocks me. Lacy runs down the stairs with some bars and a banana, and we scurry out the front door.

We jump back into her parents' convertible, and Lacy revs the engine. "I think you look great," I offer, unsure of what to say. Lacy smiles at me and hands me a banana. We ride back to the field in silence.

At sixteen, I am not sure of much. But I do know that no amount of pretty things can make up for ugly insides.

O O O

We are a culture obsessed with health. Americans spend $30 billion a year on out-of-pocket health expenses.[1] And what it means to be healthy today is a constantly moving target. One minute it's green juices and yoga, the next it's HIIT workouts and protein.

Navigating the constantly shifting messages around what it means to be healthy is overwhelming and hard to stay on top of.

But what about mental health?

What is true is that so much of our focus on health has to do with the physical body. Women and girls are bombarded by images from a very young age of scantily clad, underweight models as the pinnacle of wellness. There's no avoiding the message that skinny means healthy for the American woman. For men, it's bulging muscles and tiny tanks à la Dwayne "The Rock" Johnson (whom I love—but still).

Whether you fit this model or not, when we think of health, we think of it as something predominantly physical: eating broccoli and jogging, veiny biceps or skinny jeans. We skimp on dinner so we can have that drink at happy hour, and we say no to dessert unless we've had a salad for dinner or hit the gym earlier that day. We consume protein powders, supplements, and fresh-pressed juices with unwavering devotion.

We wait until we have an actual manifestation of a problem— a concerning lump, continued bleeding, depressive or suicidal thoughts, rapid weight gain or loss, and so on—before we advocate for our own health and shift our consciousness to the internal.

By the time our problems are physical, we have bypassed an entire series of messages from our mental, energetic, and spiritual selves that have been overtly trying to grab our attention.

While we hear about all the superfoods we must eat and exercises to try, the only thing we hear about mental health is the horrifying statistics. One in four adults suffers from a diagnosable mental health issue per year.[2] In the United States, 10.3 million adults have serious thoughts of suicide. Depression in youth has increased 5 percent in the last six years.[3] And this is only scraping the surface.

If we're not mentally and emotionally well, no matter what our external circumstance may be, we are rotting from this inside out. We've all seen people with loads of money, beauty, and even fame lose it all because they were sick on the inside.

On the flip side, if we're lucky, we've gained perspective from people who have next to nothing, yet somewhere deep inside, there is a source of light that shines through their very smile as they grin at us.

But what does it mean to be emotionally well? What does it mean to be mentally healthy? The answers are highly subjective and differ for each individual. But what is absolutely true is if you are not mentally and emotionally well, you are suffering.

No one teaches us how to be mentally or emotionally healthy. Nowhere are we taught how to handle loneliness, disappointment, rejection, fear, or our constantly ruminating thoughts. We learn by experience. This has the potential to be enlightening but often can be stifling.

We grow up with parents who have their own set of mental and emotional challenges and successes. We either model them or act in spite of their behaviors. We unknowingly create emotional legacies that pass throughout our family trees for generations based on both our empowering emotions and our disempowering, unprocessed ones.

Empowering and healthy emotions are wonderful to pass along. But as for the darker patterns, until someone in the family decides to do the work and make a change, we unconsciously carry these unwanted emotional habits with us, sharing them with each subsequent generation.

In order to further understand our own picture of mental health, we need to explore how emotion works. We experience emotion often as a result of external stimuli. For example, when something outside of you delights you—let's say a smile from a baby—you have an actual physiological response.

The brain releases serotonin and dopamine, two hormones (among others) associated with joy. This causes the other systems in the body to respond, too, making your happiness a total body experience. The autonomic nervous system kicks in, your breathing deepens, and you find yourself unavoidably grinning and feeling euphoric and pleasurable. This is just one example.

As a result of every interaction, behavior, pattern, or experience, neural pathways are created in the brain and held in the subconscious mind. What we experience early on in our lives and more frequently throughout our lives leaves deeper and stronger grooves in the brain. Therefore, if we frequently experience joy and happiness, these grooves are well run in the brain, and the body responds accordingly.

However, if we are regularly triggered by our environment to experience anger, and this was a common way of operating in our household when we were young, these will be the deepest grooves in our brains. Anger, of course, has an entirely different response in the body. Stress hormones activate, and the body responds: blood pressure rises, breathing becomes short and shallow, and our thoughts become singularly focused on the trigger.

What's more, as humans, we don't even have to interact with what is external to set off this physiological chain reaction. We merely think of a happy or horrible time and relive it in our bodies and our minds fire the same neurons to take us down the path we've practiced.

If we experience an emotion frequently enough, we begin to have feelings or mental ideas about that particular stimulus that caused said emotion. For example, let's say your boss didn't smile at you in the hall, and you now feel tense and nervous (emotion). *He's a total asshole anyway*, you tell yourself (feeling). Feelings then turn into moods, moods turn into dispositions, and dispositions become personalities. This is how our emotional legacy is created and sustained.

EMOTION ➡ FEELING ➡ MOOD ➡ DISPOSITION ➡ PERSONALITY

Habitually disempowering emotions are like metaphysical scar tissue, woven together, knotted, and deeply embedded into our unconscious. Thick, fibrous, and impenetrable, these wounds can stay buried for generations without proper attention.

Though our emotions feel rigid and fixed, accurate and strong, they are a result of habitual conditioning. The beauty of knowing this is that at any time, our emotional programming can be changed.

But do our lives allow space for us to uncover these kinds of critical, personal understandings? Are we held in an environment that encourages us to do the work required to make these life-altering shifts for ourselves and our spawn?

Not at all.

Seeing your patterns is not always easy to do in daily life. Uncovering gold like this requires contemplation, introspection, and reflective practices such as journaling, deep reading, and quiet time. But these are not typical practices many of us go to when we have more enticing options just sitting in our pockets waiting to be scrolled. Author Nicholas G. Carr suggests in his book *The Shallows* that our very behavior as a result of the technological revolution is literally changing our brains.

In an interview, Carr asserts that we are generally diminishing our power to concentrate. He goes on to say that even when we turn off our computers, because of neuroplasticity, our brains adapt to crave constant distraction and stimulus because that's what we're so used to on a given day.

We've become better at multitasking but less creative and less able to think deeply and creatively. While technology progresses, Carr suggests, humans regress. As the brain grows dependent on phone technology, the intellect weakens.[4]

Author Adam Alter seconds some of Carr's ideology in his book *Irresistible*. Alter discusses the idea of behavioral addiction that is so prevalent in our society today regarding our phones. Forty-one percent of adults experience some form of behavioral addiction, Alter says. And this was a result of a study in 2011 (iPhone 12 wasn't even out yet, y'all!). Sixty percent of adults sleep with their iPhones, and half of us check our phones during the middle of the night, Alter says.[5]

And doing so gives us that same dopamine hit that we received from the happy baby giving us her gummy grin. With instant gratification like this, who needs anything else besides the latest phone or video game? What's more, how could we possibly see the underpinnings of why we might be unhappy, struggling, or dissatisfied when our brains are conditioned for the quick fix and constantly searching for ways to fill any moment of stillness we have?

If we're all addicted to our phones and we're dumbing down our brains as a result of how distracted we are because of them, it's difficult to find space or motivation to delve deeper into this work that is so essential for mental and emotional wellness. This is why adding retreats into our lives as a regular practice is so critical to balance this normalized pace of toxicity. Retreat is what interrupts these patterns and allows us to again find balance.

Yet it's not just our mental and emotional health that is crying out for our attention these days. Our energy and how to manage it has as much to do with wellness as our mental and emotional health.

Chapter 6

ENERGETIC HEALTH

In every culture and in every medical tradition before ours,
healing was accomplished by moving energy.
—Albert Szent-Györgyi

I've always sought what makes me lift my head up, open my eyes,
and smile at what's before me. Usually, it's experiences that draw
me in—new places, fascinating conversations, natural wonders.

But when I meet my husband for the first time, I realize I'm
making the same motions and feeling the same feelings of awe.
He is 6'5", has bright-blue eyes and dimples, and is a college
basketball player. He makes fun of my capri pants when we first
start talking. A bold move, I think, as I giggle at his affront. He's
good-looking, and I like his sense of humor.

It is summertime, and my best high school friend, Allie, and I
drive down to Denver from Boulder to meet him and his friend.
They go to college with her during the school year. I've never met
them before but am excited to go do something fun with Allie.

The four of us have dinner together and laugh about embar-
rassing moments and talk about our first years in college. The
night ends quickly, and we have to leave to drive back to Boulder.

Allie and I get stuck in the parking garage because we don't have
enough cash to pay the parking ticket. Luke sees us stuck, comes
running up with his friend, and gives us forty dollars so we can go
home. It's quite a gesture for a bunch of broke college kids. He's
such a gentleman. *I wish I met more guys like him*, I remember thinking.

We go back to our separate lives and separate colleges. Luke
begins to call me when he's home from New York on break. We
develop an easy friendship over the phone. We haven't expressed
any interest in each other—at this point, neither of us is even sure.

What I do know is that he will be in my life in some capacity. I've never met a guy like Luke, so ambitious and directed in his goals. So consistent in his attention with me. There's a charge between us, a pull that no matter the states between us or other relationships we dabble in, we continue to stay close.

We're super different. He is tall and angular with sharp features where I am smaller and round. He studies business and follows the stock market. I spend my days engrossed in literature, philosophy, and pedagogy. He's a frat boy, and I am a grungy hippie. He wants to create an empire, and I want to see and change the world.

Our ideas about our futures are vastly different but share the same frequency. It's as if the energy of our dreams has the same depth and sense of passion. Maybe, just maybe it would make sense . . .

Our sophomore year in college, I go on my break to visit Allie at Cornell. The two of us have been planning and saving for my visit for over a year. I can't wait. I know I will see Luke too.

Allie's sorority has a dance, and Luke comes. We drink too much and dance the night away. I leave with Allie. Luke is dating someone else, and I am too. Something about him feels right to me, but the timing is off.

Allie and I drive to New York City the next day, just the two of us. She buys a trendy jacket, and I buy some hiking shorts. We eat the best pizza we've ever had. We lose ourselves in Chinatown and tiny shops and restaurants and in the thousands of people. We love every minute.

When we return, there's an email waiting for me from Luke. "I'm ending it with the other girl. I want to be with you." These are the only words I remember.

My relationship back home is already fizzling. There's an energy about Luke that I want in my future because it mirrors the truth of my own. Something about who he is feels steady, ambitious, and kind. With him, I feel completely safe but also open, like I can do anything at all in the world I dream of. I can picture him in my life ten, twenty, thirty years later. I tell him I plan to end my relationship too. I want to give us a try.

I go back to college in Colorado, and we spend three years in a long-distance relationship.

Now twenty years, three kids, a house, and three dogs later, trusting that energetic pull is still one of the most important decisions I've made in my life.

O O O

Understanding our own energy, how it works, and how to open to it is one of the most profound spiritual practices we can bring awareness to. Every single thought, action, emotion, and experience in our lives is an expression of energy. Energy is what breathes animation into us. Even if we live our lives from low-energy states—tired, depressed, anxious—at the core of every one of us is that soft hum of electricity: energy.

Eastern philosophies and traditions have had a handle on energy as health for centuries. Yogis spoke about the chakras, or energetic centers, Chinese healers knew about the power of chi, and Indian sages taught about Shakti, or primordial cosmic energy.

Go to a doctor in the East, and they'll look for the life force in your eyes, the fire in your belly, and the strength of your pulse to determine your vitality. You'll leave with breath work exercises to move stagnant energy and herbs to quell the heat in your gut. Ancient cultures knew that complete health comes from the inside out.

We're just catching up here in the West. It's as if because we can't see it, smell it, feel it, taste it, or hear it, energy gets less credibility when considering health. What's more, most people are completely confused about how to access their own energy.

When I lead retreats, I often ask participants where they believe our energy comes from. The most common answer I hear is that energy comes from *food*, followed second by *sleep*. Sure, you can feel more alive when you're properly rested and fed. But energy is an unending source to which we have access at all times. It's a matter of learning how to tap into and open to it.

What ancient cultures believed about energy is that it was divine, the very force of life flowing through us. The definition of Shakti—*primordial cosmic energy*—implies that energy is not quite as personal or microscopic as we choose to make it.

In other words, energy is in us and surrounding us constantly. It moves through us, using our bodies as instruments for its expression. And it carries on long after we're gone. It changes states, certainly, but it never leaves completely.

We have the opportunity to flavor this energy based on our habit patterns and wellness or the lack of it. But to say we have "no energy" is an inaccurate and overly used dictum that comes from a grave misunderstanding of our own potential at any given moment. It's more of a problem in thinking, conditioning, and relating with our source.

Our greatest power comes from opening ourselves up to that which is beyond our egoic selves, acting as a vessel for the infinite potential energy. It's as if there are two selves: a *Big me* and a *little me*.

Little me is consumed with the self—personal success or discomforts, pain or pleasure. *Little me* resists energy that creates pain and attaches to energy that creates pleasure. *Little me*'s exchange with energy is conditional and shifts based on circumstance. *I am open if I like it; I am closed if I don't.*

But *Big me* is unfazed by discomfort on the personal level. *Big me* lives from higher purpose and infinite potential. *Big me* knows that no matter the blow, we remain open because there is a lesson here. *Big me* knows it is *through* our problems that we sculpt our souls and evolve. And we cannot attach to or reject either pleasure or pain in order to live our brightest *Big me* lives. This energy is meant to move through that which is open.

The internal turmoil and personal problems of our lifetime come as a result of closing ourselves off to energy and living purely from *little me*. *Little me* clings and resists that which does not serve it: *I like him, but I hate her. I am this, but I am not that.*

When we become overly attached to what something means to *little me*, we are blinded and cannot access *Big me* like we once could. When we have emotional pain, either passed down or newly created, the tendency is to close down. This creates a tightness or blockage, both in the body and in the spirit. This influences how we move in the world.

Let's say a friend excluded you from a party she had in high school. As a result, you felt left out and unpopular. Each time you saw her in the halls at school, you were reminded of how unpopular you felt. You saw her so often; she began to serve as a trigger for how you felt about yourself.

Time passes, and you start to now think of yourself as unliked by the masses. Your energy takes on a viscous and dark quality when others are around you. They feel the weight of your energetic pain body by just standing in your presence. You speak in a way that mirrors this energy. And you send out signals of "*I just want to be alone!*" even though this couldn't be further from the truth. You've just blocked and negatively sculpted the energy that you're emitting out to the world.

You go off to college, still carrying this blocked energy that you've attached to and now identified with. Groups of people gather to meet each other at the start of school, but you avoid groups because you believe you're unpopular. As a result, you are alone and have created a self-fulfilling prophecy.

The high school friend from long ago had red hair, so now every time you see someone with red hair, you are a little bit skeptical of his or her character. Furthermore, even though you know she went to college in another state, your heart starts to race, and your palms start to sweat every time you see a redheaded woman at the store, fearing it's her.

Years later, you move back to your hometown. You bump into your redheaded ex-friend in the store. She is pleasant and kind and delighted to see you, to your surprise. You suddenly feel silly for all the years you spent hating the gingers of the world. You may or may not recognize that your tendency to isolate yourself comes from that very energetic thought that you identified with. That was yours. It had nothing to do with her.

This is what it looks like to close down and overly personalize energy that needs to move. Creating sticky energy that's meant to be fluid only hurts the host. Energy is your gift to use, not your possession to claim or resist. Unfinished energy patterns create who you are, and if you're not careful, they can completely run your life.

So how then do you stay open? It is the practice of a lifetime. Making your ability to stay open dependent on conditional, external stimuli is to allow for ultimate suffering and complete lack of personal control. When you let that which is outside of you influence your feelings about yourself and your energy, it's no wonder you feel depressed, anxious, fearful, and depleted all the time.

In order to stay open, you must find something solid in you, a core, a connection to *Big me*, and remind yourself over and over again that no matter what happens, *"I am a vessel through which divinity flows to myself and others."*

The greatest moments in our lives, the highest states that we've ever achieved, are as a result of how open we were to this flow. Think back and see if you can remember one of the greatest moments of your life. Ask yourself, *How open was I then?* I'd be willing to bet that in each of those great moments, you allowed yourself to be truly open and had limited expectations. Remember these experiences, and remind yourself what remaining open offers you.

You can familiarize yourself with your expansive, unconditional, *Big me* self through the practice of meditation. There are countless styles, teachers, programs, apps, and more that support the practice of meditation today. But perhaps my favorite frame of meditation is given by my meditation teacher, Chhoje Tulku Rinpoche.

He says meditation is the practice of "making friends with yourself." Many Westerners come to meditation with the determination and outcome-based mindset that makes the practice a major effort and misses the point entirely. I love the lightness of the idea of making friends with ourselves and the notion that it is meant to be just this gentle.

Meditation can be broken down into two main categories: form meditation and formless meditation.

- *Form meditation:* In form meditation, we focus on something aside from just allowing our thoughts to move through us. It may be an audio recording, visualization, walking meditation, mantra, our breath, or a candle.

- *Formless meditation:* In formless meditation, we merely notice a thought as it comes, we label it "thought," and we let it go. We become skilled at letting thoughts move through us, and we remember we are the observer behind the thoughts. This is also known as *Shamatha* meditation, "peaceful abiding" or mindfulness meditation.

Whichever method you choose, it is the practice of sitting still, slowing down, and being with yourself and your energy. You sit to know yourself so you can condition yourself to live from the inside out. Our brains are like puppies, active and unruly, and if left unattended, they can be completely out of control. We can train them to sit and be still, or we can be dominated by them.

In the practice of meditation, you go against your habitual need to constantly do, think, plan, analyze, and more. Meditation brings you beyond the analytical mind. You break this pattern by sitting on your chair or cushion and staying with yourself, despite distractions.

Meditation teaches you to soften your gripping or resisting. Bring your gaze and focus inward. Otherwise, if you become solely identified with your external world, you will forever be a victim to that which happens outside of you.

In meditation, you develop your inner muscle. You create ground in yourself, so the external groundlessness doesn't knock you down quite so much. The most benefit comes from regular and consistent practice. Even ten minutes per day can make a major impact on your awareness and sense of presence and gratitude.

It is in meditation where you condition yourself to disidentify with your thoughts that come and go, like the waves of an ocean. You become the witness that's behind the thought, knowing that you are the one who watches.

In this way, you become more comfortable letting energy move through you because you don't see yourself *as* that particular energetic thought or emotion. This allows you to be less reactive in daily interactions because you know your thoughts are transient and can change if you desire. No need to get all worked up.

Building this relationship takes time and effort. This is exactly what takes place on retreat. If we spend our entire lives awhirl in our mental obscurations and bound to the material world of pleasure and pain, how on earth will we build our emotional and energetic muscles?

Developing a healthy relationship with ourselves requires time, meditation, introspective practice, and commitment to truth, just as in building an intimate relationship with another. And finding our *Big me* and living from him or her is not only worth stepping away for; it is essential for living a positive inner life for the duration of our precious human lives.

Chapter 7

SPIRITUAL HEALTH

We are not human beings having a spiritual experience. We are spiritual beings having a human experience.
— Pierre Teilhard de Chardin, *Writings*

There are nineteen of us in my study abroad program. After traveling for over thirty-six hours, we arrive in Kathmandu, Nepal. None of us knows each other, aside from the few hellos we exchanged before our long flight.

We sit on the bus gazing out the window in shock at the scenes of Kathmandu: cows walking across the street, homeless children who have children begging for food, local people bending over to relieve themselves in the street, and the overwhelming stench. A combined odor of garbage, Nepalese spices, and fecal matter singes our nose hairs.

We're headed to Pharping, a quiet Newari town on the outskirts of the Kathmandu Valley about an hour away, to begin our program. We finally arrive, and it's a welcome change from the big city. Surrounded by rice terraces and sounds of rooster crows, we unload our giant, fancy American bags.

We're split into small groups and asked to go around the town and connect with people. We learn a few small Nepali pleasantries—how to order tea, how to say please and thank you—and we're on our way.

This is my first time leaving my home country. To say that I am still in shock is an understatement. Being here makes me feel embarrassed by our collective wealth compared to the people in this village. Entire families live in one room, wooden shacks.

Some have tarps, some don't. None has running water. I wonder what they'll think of us walking around in our Patagonia jackets and never-before-worn hiking boots we purchased for this trip.

Our teachers suggest we don't take pictures of people unless we ask them first. They suggest we connect with people here and be mindful not to objectify them. Nevertheless, a girl in my group snaps a pic without asking. A deep feeling of shame settles in my core, and I wish I was doing this walk alone. *These people are not an exhibit,* I think to myself.

Even so, everywhere we walk, children come out and yell, "Hi! Hi! Hello!" at the top of their lungs and follow us down the tiny dirt paths. Men and women are quick to smile and give us the namaste, and we swiftly learn to do the same. Nepalese people are easy to fall in love with, so fast to offer smiles and *chiya* to strange Americans looming about.

There is a temple in town, Dakshinkali Temple. It's a famous Hindu pilgrimage site where the locals worship Kali, the goddess of death and destruction, by sacrificing live animals. It just so happens we arrived the night before a ceremony. Our teachers invite us to wake early in the morning to witness it.

Many of us are torn about whether to go. At twenty, I'm a vegetarian and not particularly interested in witnessing the killing of goats for worship. It seems so far out of my realm of normal.

Yet this is something that's important to these people here, who after only twenty-four hours already intrigue me. Something in me is pulled to witness this ceremony. So I wake up early the next morning with a few other students and head to the ceremony.

There are so many people it's hard to get close to the temple, where the sacrifice takes place. What is clear is that the animals know what's happening. Goats pull hard on their owner's ropes to get away as they are yanked toward the inner temple. We stand perched up on the side of a hill, watching as best we can.

I can't see the blade, but I can see the blood. Loads of it spilling across the white, marble temple floors. Two women roll around in it in some kind of trance and say things I can't understand. I am at once transfixed and horrified. They chant and pray, and my mouth hangs open, and I hold my hand to my heart.

I have witnessed some kind of transformation during this experience, and in some way, I too am changed. It's as if in ten minutes, my eyes are more open than they have been in the past twenty years of my life.

We climb back up to our guesthouse in the same silence we shared on the bus. At dinner that night, we make toasts to each other, to the beginning of our program, and to the goats that sit in some kind of golden curry atop the plates in front of us.

We are always dying and being reborn again. I gaze at the goat atop my plate amid the vibrant Nepali dancers who initiate our program while we sip *raksi* and chuckle in our drunkenness. It's been four years since I've touched meat, but somehow, eating a bite of it right here, right now, feels right. I join the group in toasts and prayer and eat my delicious Nepali curry.

An unforgettable end to ignite a life-altering beginning.

O O O

What it means to be spiritual varies widely from person to person. Unquestionably, how we define spiritual health is open to interpretation. Like a snowflake, it is precisely unique for every last person. For some, spirituality has a religious connotation. For others, religion has nothing to do with it. And some want nothing to do with spirituality at all.

What is clear is that our beliefs about the value of organized religion, as a society, are shifting. US church membership has fallen significantly in the last two decades. The percentage of Americans who report belonging to a church, synagogue, or mosque was at 50 percent in 2018, down from 70 percent in the 1990s. Since the turn of the century, the percentage of US adults with no religious affiliation has more than doubled.[1]

It's evident that as a collective, we hold less and less scheduled space, time, or tradition for matters of the spirit. Individually, sure. Perhaps within certain communities more than others.

These days, we substitute therapists for priests and life coaches for rabbis. But what implications do these shifting values have on our inner lives and understanding of ourselves?

Some studies posit that religious people are happier and live longer than the rest of the world. One of the most comprehensive studies, published in JAMA Internal Medicine in 2016, found that women who attended any kind of religious service more than once per week had a 33 percent lower chance of dying in a sixteen-year follow-up study than their nonreligious peers. Another study, published in *PLOS One* in 2018, found in an eighteen-year follow-up study that regular-attending worshipers were 55 percent less likely to die than people who didn't frequent religious services.[2]

It's unclear if this is a result of the community benefits associated with going to weekly services or the religious teachings themselves. However, the studies are significant enough to make us stop to wonder what we can glean from them.

Joseph Campbell, prolific American author and professor of religion and mythology, believed that you can tell what a society values by the size of the buildings erected in its honor. For centuries, the largest and most impressive buildings were places of worship—Notre Dame, Boudhanath Stupa, Angkor Wat, the Egyptian pyramids.

In some places in the world, this still holds true. But for America these days, our most striking structures are now dedicated to commerce, with a side of sporting events. Worldwide—from Abu Dhabi, Shanghai, Malaysia, and NYC—the massive skyscrapers tell the story of what matters today: capitalism. How we spend our time and mental energy models this value.

So what then of our inner lives and our contemplative practices? Society used to value contemplative thinkers as an important function in society; they were individuals who helped us evolve as a collective. But as our structures suggest, and as our pursuit of individual success continues, it's apparent our values have changed.

Where do we make space for ceremony and ritual? Do these even hold value anymore? Certainly, these primal ways of relating to ourselves and others can still offer us something. But how? Where?

Religious or not, leading a life filled with purpose and meaning is a common yearning among humankind. We want to be useful, be connected, and feel like our lives mean something.

Further still, we want to feel like we lived a life that was true to who we are. The number one regret of the dying is, *I wish I'd had the courage to live a life true to myself, not the life others expected of me.*[3] Imagine lying on your death bed feeling like you never really lived your truth. Surely there's a better way.

To touch this truth, we have to think bigger than our *little me* selves that exist in the everyday. Whether it's God or spirit, nature or source, that which is beyond the five senses, that which has always been and always will be, yearns for us to see our own light.

Our lives are often so busy, distracted, full, and also beautiful that we forget to pick our heads up. It is only in pulling away from our habitual routines when we again see the bigger picture of our own lives. We gaze with a bird-like perspective on our circumstances back home and uncover new understandings of who we are and what we want, things that before were impossible to see.

When we pull away from the rushing current of life for retreat, seemingly random people come into our lives, offering us messages along the way. A new career inspiration pops into our heads in morning meditation, or a relationship intuition comes to the forefront of our minds on our hike. Dreams carry messages from loved ones we've lost, and books we read shift the way we think about our children or parents or friends. Upholding a new routine on retreat makes us reconsider the way we spend our time back home. Perhaps it is God, the universe, nature, or source communicating to us, as it always has. Only now, in the quiet of retreat, we can hear it.

In our daily lives, we believe we know so firmly who we are. We settle into this construct and act and live without questioning the fluidity of our nature. Pulling away for retreat and stepping out of our comfort zones allow us to again access this essential mutability and open our minds and hearts to be something other than what we previously so assuredly thought we were.

Just as when I was a young woman in Nepal witnessing the ceremony that in my previous experience would in no way be considered "spiritual," in an instant, retreating can help us shift our view. Witnessing the devout find meaning in the sacrifice felt like I was being let into something ancient and shared. And despite my strong views about being vegetarian then, refusing the meat that night based on my prior opinions felt rude and somehow wrong in a third world country where, as an initiatory offering, they shared with me their finest delicacy.

It was a present moment decision. One that I wouldn't have made in my typical life back home. One that I might have even judged. Yet stepping outside of my comfort zone allowed me space to redefine who I thought I was. It allowed me to fully experience what was before me. The experience, not the idea or label. This kind of pulling away allows us to be more intentional and present.

What's true about presence is that it is moment by moment, an evolution. It's not wedded to patterns, titles, and predictable structures. Presence has the potential to be absolutely anything. Retreating reminds us of this and plops us right back into presence.

As a result, we can go home with a wider view of who we are and what is possible in our lives. It's difficult to get this viewpoint otherwise. These retreat resets allow us to craft our conditions with much more precision and intention because we had a pause to pay attention—and the reminder that we can be or do anything despite how we may have been living prior.

Like an artist, ever aware of the value of negative space in her explosively vibrant painting, it is only in making that *negative space* in our lives, in honoring that quiet, that we can again hear the signs that remind us to see how brightly our lives shine when we are in them.

My message is simply this: that we make space for space. And that every now and again, we leave our daily constructs. To add to our beautiful and full portraits we call life, we do as the transcendentalists did. We allow ourselves to regularly pull away for no other reason than to hear our own voices once again. And we can blur the lines of who we are right now and rediscover who we'd like to be going forward. This is what retreating offers us.

Retreating offers value not always for its own sake but for once we return home afterward. For it is during our retreat that we make spiritual leaps that then manifest into physical form when we come home. When we return after our retreats, with a steady heart and a surefootedness in our own divinity, neither crowd nor chaos can sway us. It is we who, again, are in charge of the sway.

Chapter 8

LIFE
AS LAB

Life is a good teacher and a good friend. Things are always in
transition, if we could only realize it. Nothing ever sums itself
up in the way that we like to dream about. The off-center, the
in-between state is an ideal situation, a situation in which we
don't get caught and we can open our hearts and minds beyond
limit.

—Pema Chödrön, *When Things Fall Apart*

My husband and I are participating in a weeklong seminar about
how to uplevel our lives, personally and professionally. We are on
day two, and after an incredibly long and fruitful day one, we are
wide eyed and ready to go.

There are five thousand people at this event, and my husband and I were assigned to sit in different sections. Last night,
the conference let out at two o'clock in the morning. We were so
amped up, it didn't seem to matter. Now, on the second night, it is
two o'clock, and the speaker shows no sign of slowing.

Back home, I am a nine-thirty-to-bed kind of person. There
is not a chance that will happen this week. I tell myself I am fine
with it. But the tiredness starts to weigh heavily on me, and my
eyes start to droop.

I see my husband a few sections away, sitting on the edge of
his seat, fully engaged. I look at my workshop partner and tell
her I don't think I can make it. I put my head on her shoulder
and almost fall asleep right there.

I look back to Luke and contemplate what to do. If I go and
grab him and tell him I need to drive back to the hotel, he'll have

to leave too. But if I stay here, I will full-out fall asleep. I look to him and feel bad. But not as bad as I feel tired.

"OK!" the speaker says. "Time to get on your feet! Only two more items to cover, and you can head out for the night!"

Holy crap, I. Can. Not. Handle. This. Two more?! I thought surely we were close to finishing. I get up and go over to my husband without another thought. He is wide eyed and bushy tailed and excited for the next bit of content.

"I'm so sorry," I say, "but I'm just dying here. We have to go."

"You sure you can't make it a *little* longer?" he pleads.

"No way," I say, ready to get the heck out of there.

The car ride home is silent. He is disappointed. I can feel it in the silence. And I am so tired, I can't quite care as much as I should. I start to feel annoyed by this whole conference to begin with.

It's only day two. From what we know, every single night goes this long. I want to go back to my comfortable bed at home, go back to where it's warm in my house (it's literally *freezing* inside at the conference to keep people awake), and eat the food that I want to eat. I'm super passionate about health and my routine, and this is messing with *all* of it! I can't make it through five more days of this.

"I just don't know if this is for me," I say to break the silence in the car. "I mean, I like the content, but I feel like this whole experience is just not worth it. Besides, I am constantly reading and learning this kind of stuff already on my own."

More silence.

"Do you really feel that way?" he asks gloomily. I realize in this moment that this conference that we have been waiting for months to come to may pull us apart more than it brings us together. The exact opposite of what we wanted.

"I do," I say without hesitation.

We wake up the next morning, and I feel bad. I hop into the shower and try to pump myself up for the day, but it feels forced. How on earth am I going to do this again for another eighteen hours today? I can't even imagine it.

And then something hits me. Standing in the shower, as the water hits my skin, I realize my pattern. *This* is what I do. Every time I am challenged or uncomfortable or don't like something, I push away and say, "This is not for me. I don't need this" or "I can figure out how to do all this myself."

Sure, this is a good response sometimes—a way to set healthy boundaries and advocate for my own needs. But has it kept me away from things that might actually be good for me? Absolutely. In an instant, I unlock my pattern and realize that there is more for me here.

Oh my gosh! I think to myself. *I get it! I get it! I got a nugget I can work with now.* I get out of my cathartic shower elated. I tell Luke what I realized about myself and that because of my pattern, I almost created a circumstance that would have drawn us apart.

But now I can choose to stay in it despite my resistance. He is relieved, and so am I. We hop into the car for the day, both energized, open, and ready for more.

And now I have a powerful lesson for next time I am stuck and to take with me for the rest of the conference and, more importantly, my life.

o o o

One of the greatest confusions about health is that we need something external to "fix" ourselves. We need certain memberships, the most well-known teachers, the freshest gear, and a constant variety of healing tactics and ideas to grow into our best selves.

The great truth about retreat is all we need is ourselves. Aside from relaxing and breaking patterns from our daily roles and routines, retreat allows us to be self-scientists. And with regular retreating, we learn that there is no need for fixing because nothing is broken. When we retreat, we learn to better understand ourselves and others. We then make supportive shifts, not with unprocessed aggression but with intention.

We use what arises on retreat as our petri dish, and we watch to see what unfolds in our own consciousness and before our eyes. *This* is where our most profound lessons and breakthroughs lie.

But even before this, we allow ourselves the time to just relax. We relax the mind, we relax the body, and as a result, our energy shifts.

We connect at first to our basic needs. It sounds funny, but women have such a strange relationship with our basic needs. We have an incredible relationship with our feelings and are able to connect to our sense of spirit almost immediately. But we often forgo our own needs for the sake of others. This stems from that need to constantly be pleasing. Can you think of a time when you've skipped a meal or a shower in order to take care of something for someone else? I bet so.

So an essential step for a woman to rebuild her energy on retreat is to reconnect to her basic needs. You get plenty of sleep. You eat when you notice your body feels hungry. You take regular showers or baths. You do the things that feel nurturing, healing, compassionate, and essential first.

Once you have settled down from your frenetic energy, you start to dig into the work of retreat. You create a schedule for yourself, adopt new and supportive routines and habits, and drop yourself into this new container.

Immediately, messages start to show themselves to you. There will be pieces of your day you relish—hiking, journaling, reading, getting a full night's rest. And there will be parts of your time that challenge you deeply—how your body aches from long sustained meditation, staying silent, and yearning for internet access. Different Elements trigger or inspire different participants.

The questions become, *What did* you *uncover about* you? *And how can this help you going forward?* Just because meditation feels long and uncomfortable does not mean you skip it and opt for more hikes, since those feel nice and slightly easier. Lean into what challenges you knowing there is a message waiting for you on the other side of that resistance.

As a self-scientist, you learn that resistance is often your greatest teacher. This is how you sculpt and strengthen your spirit. If you never have opponents, you have no idea what you're capable of. You realize that the challenges are where the growth lies.

So when something feels difficult, you relax.

Let go of your ideas and expectations about who you are, what you need, and how you normally do things. Allow your fixed ideals to soften to make way for a more evolved and present-moment self. One that, eventually, you can take back home and share with those around you.

Because you're in an entirely new environment running an entirely new set of patterns, you can't help but learn things about yourself. Your likes and dislikes for what you're doing on your retreat are the first whispers of self-understanding.

What does this mean about me?

What does this have to teach me?

How can I grow from this?

Just as a scientist does, you collect data throughout your retreat. Record it in your journal, and see if you feel the same tomorrow and the next day. This is the exact information you need at this time. There is no practice of presence like retreating.

The reactions, challenges, emotions, dreams, thoughts, insights, and breakthroughs from this very retreat are what you need to make your next most important hypothesis about your life. This is how you start to find a new pace and reestablish the relationship with your inner voice again. It is always there and has always been there. But sometimes it becomes deeply quieted in your hurried home life.

This voice is worth finding again. It is the voice that always knows. It is the *Big me* that is not the ever-fluctuating emotion and can give you the truth, inspiration, and healing when you are back home too.

So use your life as a laboratory while on retreat, and become a self-scientist of the greatest kind. This way, you come out with discoveries that can change your world once you reenter it.

Chapter 9

SELF-CARE IS NOT SELFISH

I want to think again of dangerous and noble things.
I want to be light and frolicsome.
I want to be improbable beautiful and afraid of nothing.
As though I had wings.

—Mary Oliver, *Owls and Other Fantasies*

I stop at the store on my way out of town to pick up some snacks for the road. This is my first weekend away by myself after having my second child, and I'll be going to my favorite Colorado town for retreating: Crestone. I grab some apples and a nut mix, some chips, and a few Bobo's bars. I am ready to go.

I amble up to the checkout counter. I feel light and free. The crushing guilt of leaving ceased the moment I walked out my door at home, thankfully. I feel like myself again at the grocery store, all alone like this. It is a relief.

In line I see an old neighbor I grew up near as a child. I knew her in the way most children know their adult neighbors—which is to say not very well. We say hello. She is friendly and offers smiles as we share typical pleasantries.

I tell her about my parents and my young children; she tells me about her husband, whose face I vaguely remember. He is having back problems. *We are all aging*, I think to myself as snapshot memories of her house pop into my mind from decades ago, my brothers and I hiding in her backyard during nighttime games of kick the can.

"Headed somewhere fun?" she asks inquisitively, noticing my arms bursting with car snacks.

"Yeah, I'm going on retreat for a weekend by myself. I thought it would be good to have some time away for myself." As I speak, I begin to lower my voice and look downward. It is not a work trip. It is not a family trip. It is just for me, alone. Though moments ago I felt so confident, I suddenly feel unsure about my decision to leave as I recount it to her.

"A retreat, huh? Who is watching your young kids?" She is playful in her exchange with me. She doesn't know that her prodding is touching my deepest fear.

Am I selfish?

Am I a bad mom?

She is smiling, and I am now riddled with guilt that only moments ago was nowhere to be found. She nods, perplexed by what I'm saying.

"Women today!" she says with a tone of sarcasm. "You have so many needs!" We say goodbye, and I scurry off to the car with my snacks. *She was just trying to be funny*, I remind myself as I throw my things in the passenger seat.

And I sit down and try to get the penetrating guilt to dissipate.

o o o

It never fails, every single time I decide to go on retreat and share my intentions out loud, someone will say something like, "Must be nice," or "Wow, you have a really nice husband to let you get away with that!" or "I could *never* go away just for myself."

At first, I feel bad. For a moment, I question what I'm doing. I wonder if maybe they're right. But the inside me, the real me, *Big me*, knows how incredibly wrong they are.

"You should do it too," I often say back.

We love to keep people in predictable roles because it makes us feel good about the boxes we've formed around ourselves. Putting ourselves before everyone else looks selfish to people who live from outdated thinking. But even these people, especially these people, can learn from your example.

The people whom others think I am "selfishly" leaving are the very ones for whom I retreat. My children, my husband, my family, my close friends, the quality of the work I produce afterward: all see the benefits of my pulling away starting the moment I return.

But it is at first hard to go against the grain.

Perhaps you know from your own experience that when you take care of yourself, you have so much more to offer others. There is no greater intention than to give the best of yourself to your causes and the ones you love.

Our society is desperate to see people who are internally healthy and whole. These are the leaders we need in our uncertain times—one's who are vital and thriving. We are all yearning for meaning and the ability to live our truths and have our inside lives match our outside lives. Finding this meaning and sense of alignment comes from getting comfortable with and spending time with ourselves.

From time to time we lose ourselves. We forget the value of being alone with ourselves. And so we operate with our heads down, like everyone else does. We do, mindlessly.

It is not tragic. It is normal. But it quickly becomes tragic if we never question the value of always being in groups or constantly being plugged in, always giving to others, awhirl in the daily needs of work, family, community, and society.

We each are here to create and share ourselves with the world in our own ways, that only we can do—a family, a business, a volunteer position, a dance, a poem, a life.

We have to first know our own depths before we can uncover what it is we wish to bring to the surface for ourselves and for our greater world. Knowing what is true and real about our own gifts is what gives them power and endurance in a world that can easily wear us down.

In all the retreats I've taken in my life, I've never regretted a single one. The truth is, every single retreat has something new to teach me that I only discover because I took the time away. Retreating is the best way I've found to really know myself and my deepest intentions. It's my most meaningful form of self-care. It is how I access my creative wellspring. It is why my relationships thrive.

And so I invite you to your own retreat. You've read the research, and by now, you see the need.

If there's something in you that yearns for more, your time has come. Or maybe there's a slight, hard-to-identify dissatisfaction just beneath the surface that keeps you living life at 70 percent when you know you are capable of 100 percent.

A retreat is the antidote that points to how to bridge this divide. If you feel a pull, a gentle nudge for more, the time is now, Dear One.

And so I wish you well. And I welcome you to your own next level.

Part II

HOW TO GO ABOUT THE LEAVING

Chapter 10

THE LEAVING

Go because you want to. Because wanting to leave is enough.
—Cheryl Strayed, *Brave Enough*

So you've made your decision. You feel the pull for retreat, and you've committed (at least in your head) to do one. Perhaps there's excitement in the decision. Perhaps there's fear. Maybe you still can't entirely explain why you know you need or want a retreat. You just know.

This is reason enough.

Whatever it is that brings you to the recognition of this need, you must trust with unwavering devotion. This call is the whisper of the spirit, the gentle beckoning of the soul. The truth about retreat is, unless you have an agreed-upon deal with yourself—like *I go on retreat once every six months*—you'll battle internally about whether you *really* need it. You may wonder if now is *really* the best time, if you can *actually* afford it, if it will *really* do you any good.

So once you make the decision, you must take some kind of action that will commit you to your decision. Book a plane ticket, reserve a cabin in the woods, pay the deposit on an organized retreat, request for the time off, tell your partner or close friend.

This way, when you feel hesitation or regret in your decision, your action will remind you that you are already in. You've already committed. The part of you that is fearful is soothed by the part of you that was inspired. Characterize your initial insight to go as an intuitive message speaking directly to you and then drop the inner battle.

You may need some kind of approval or support before you completely commit to your retreat. You plan to take a week off, and your boss wants to know why. Or you have young children and need the support of a spouse or partner. Or you are in a relationship and want your beloved's blessing.

First off, be intentional about whom you tell. Share on a need-to-know basis. Because retreating is an inside job, we don't need the opinions of all those outside. When you share with too many people, you welcome the views of others, whether they are relevant or not. Even energetically, you receive the projections and beliefs of others when you need only to be focusing on your own. The sticky energy and opinionated views of others need not join you before or on your retreat. You'll have enough of your own work to do.

Yet for those you do tell, how you frame this conversation can be particularly important and allow for new depth of relationship, no matter the connection. If you've never taken retreat before, it can be difficult to explain to others why you want to go. Even if you've taken retreats before, people don't always understand.

We live in an outcome-driven world. People want to know, What's the point or purpose? How will this help you? What will your results be? And if they're in relationship with you, how will this affect them? Why do you feel you need to escape? Some might ask, What are you running from?

In fact, you run not from something but toward a better understanding of yourself. Expressing your desire to make space for yourself is an opportunity to redirect your intimate relationship to an even healthier course. We are taught that in coupling, especially marriage, we make decisions together. We support the unit before we support the individual.

It is my belief that to best support the unit, we support the individuals also. Having to disassociate from ourselves in order to serve a greater whole is a dangerous precedent to set. This can happen easily in families, relationships, or organizations. Where there is a high level of attachment, there is a high level of expectation. *You* must *show up for the family reunion. You* can't *be gone over Valentine's Day! No one* ever *misses the company party!*

These kinds of limiting relational beliefs will keep you trapped in unhealthy relationships and, furthermore, tight and tiny boxes that you'll spend your whole life trying to break free from.

Well-meaning people will always have expectations of you. In fact, it's the ones who are closest to you, who's subtle, often unspoken expectations are the hardest to recognize and reconcile. The question is, Will you live your life in service of them or take the wheel of your own life?

Taking your retreat is a chance to break free from the confining box of all expectations, both gentle and overt. Do it a new way. Understand that yes, your relationships are important, but the one with yourself is the *most* important. No spouse, friend, work obligation, or otherwise can take precedence over this one.

What we need desperately right now are people who are grounded in themselves, comfortable in their own skin, and practiced in matters of their minds, emotions, energies, and spirits. These are the people who will positively shape families, communities, and the greater world: those who have first learned how to do so for themselves.

So frame the conversation of your departure for retreat with certainty and with love. Use "I" statements, and do not ask for permission. Express an inner desire, one to know yourself again, to make space for yourself to flourish even more. Remind your loved ones that to better serve the greater good and also them, you must first serve yourself.

If you already have this culture in place in your relationship—be it with a supportive partner, boss, or friend—this will be smooth. But if this is a new concept in your relationship, consider yourself the path paver.

The beauty of creating this kind of nurturing ethos in your intimate relationship is that once you return, your partner can experience a retreat or personal enhancement experience of their own too. It can be a new offering you give to one another, a new way to uplevel yourselves for yourselves and also for each other. It is a beautiful freedom that sets the stage for a relationship where each person is allowed to move, grow, and change as they see fit.

Our relationships are living, breathing entities. They either shift and grow with us, or stagnate and become outdated because they cannot allow for the needs of both parties. A way to water this growing organism is to allow the spaciousness of the individual, so counterintuitive to what our world says about coupling.

Yet so essential.

So share with your partner, friend, or boss your intention, and tell him or her of your plan to return. Answer logistical questions with as much pragmatism as possible, ever assuring your partner (or yourself) that this is not about growing *beyond* anybody in particular; it is about growing *within* yourself. Again, an inside act, not an outside one.

Your partner may fear that you seek growth that doesn't involve him or her. That they will be left behind in the process. So long as you are in a healthy relationship, you can assure your partner that this is not so. Remind your beloved of your love and your intention to come back filled up with more to share.

If you are in unhealthy relationships, pulling away for retreat to find your voice and courage becomes even more essential. It is difficult to take action if you can't see with clarity what needs to shift in the first place.

In a loving and healthy relationship, a partner will see your glow after returning once from a retreat, and he or she will get it. They'll see it in your eyes and feel it in your presence; you are renewed. The greatest of partners even begin to suggest to each other, "*Maybe you should take a retreat for yourself.*" Because this is what *Big me* love looks like. Confident love—rather than dependency, enmeshment, and conditionality—allows both parties to soar.

But it doesn't entirely matter what your partner, friend, or boss says. We must train ourselves to be our own best partners. This is a spiritual practice all on its own. *Maybe I should take a retreat*, we say to ourselves.

Know this murmur to be your truth. Do it because the inspiration for leaving is more important than the comfort of staying. To stay true to your soul, you commit to leaving for retreat.

Chapter 11

GO YOUR
OWN WAY

Authenticity is a collection of choices that we have to make every day. It's about the choice to show up and be real. The choice to be honest. The choice to let our true selves be seen.
—Brené Brown, *The Gifts of Imperfection*

With so many options and different practices for doing retreat today, it can be daunting to determine which is right for you. How do you know which style will awaken the most in you? If you've retreated before, should you do the same thing every time or try something different each time?

The key to answering these and other questions that arise when you consider *how* to do your retreat is to start to get curious about your intention for retreat *right now*. Why *now?* This will help guide many of your upcoming decisions. Once you gain clarity on why you need to pull away now, it's time to begin to think more about logistics.

One primary question that will set the trajectory for how to build your personal retreat is, *Do I go alone or join a group?* The answer to this question leads to a very different set of outcomes.

While you may start with solo retreats, joining an organized retreat can be a good new flush of inspiration. Alternatively, if you always opt for joining groups when you go on retreat, you may find incredible value by structuring your own for yourself next time. Let's explore the details of both so you can see what feels like the right fit for you.

Solo Retreats

There is something enchanting about doing a retreat all by yourself—the hermit, the transcendentalist, the sage. Stepping away by yourself can be one of the fastest ways to your own inner knowing, like the masters of old times have always done.

This may or may not be true for each of us individually. But solo retreats certainly offer a powerful opportunity for transformation, particularly if you find yourself regularly surrounded by people—maybe you're raising a family or constantly surrounded by coworkers or friends. A solo retreat is a great respite from lots of crowd stimulation. If you've decided to go it alone, here are the factors to consider.

Intention

The desire to know ourselves more deeply is what drives most of us to retreat. Or maybe you just plain need a break. But thinking more sincerely about your intention can help guide some of the important decisions you will need to make before you embark on your journey.

Do you desire to create a more consistent meditation practice? Do you want to release limiting beliefs and come home with new inspiration to make big changes in your life? Are you hoping to journal, rest, and make time to listen to recorded versions of meaningful teachings? Do you just need space from the pace of life back home? (See the appendix for a comprehensive list of retreat intentions.)

Gaining clarity around your intention for retreat helps determine what kind of space you'll need as well as how to set your schedule. A person who wishes to strengthen her meditation practice will have a retreat that looks very different from someone who is looking to heal from a recent loss.

Though the retreats I guide all look different and the intentions always vary from participant to participant, I have the same objectives for every one of my retreat experiences. (See the appendix for an example of the retreat objectives I use for the retreats I host.)

But objectives are different from your intention. An intention is the overarching, umbrella reason you need a retreat in this moment. If you're clear on this, all other decisions you make will be easy. Create an intention for yourself and write it down in your journal or keep it in the forefront of your mind, and let this be the guiding force for your retreat.

My intention for retreating right now is:

_____

_____

_____

Location

Often, retreatants who want to go it alone desire a good amount of silence on their retreats. This is important to consider when choosing a location. Do you plan to stay in a monastery or a cabin in the woods? Would you like to stay close by where you live or go somewhere far away? Do you want to be completely alone in nature, or do you want other people on-site, perhaps a kitchen where meals are made, even if you aren't conversing with them? Do you desire a place with more natural or urban surroundings?

There is no particular rule when it comes to choosing a location, so long as you have a level of comfort and ease. While it may feel alluring to go into the woods and stay in a tent for your retreat, if you're dealing with constant bug bites and freezing temperatures at night, it's hard to get to the deeper layers of the psyche and allow for energetic shift.

While there are certainly lessons to learn from "toughing it out" on retreat with incredibly harsh external conditions, retreating is different from an outward-bound experience. It's an inward-bound one. In order to move past the level of the physical, you have to take care of your basic physical necessities first and foremost.

You don't need to stay at the Ritz-Carlton, but making sure you have access to food, water, shelter, and a comfortable bed and shower is important. You need not waste time and energy dwelling on basic necessities. If you ensure they are met beforehand, you'll have space to go deeper when you arrive.

When choosing your location, be sure that it can accommodate all your physical and safety needs. If you are alone in the woods, make sure someone knows the details of your itinerary in case of an emergency.

While no particular site is inherently better than another when it comes to retreating (you can do it in your basement, after all), some are certainly more conducive to transformational work. This is precisely why monasteries, hot springs, and other natural wonders, historical religious sites, and energetic vortexes can be powerful places to retreat.

Spaces that energetically or historically hold the resonance of introspective, transformational, or spiritual work can add a significant layer of impact to your daily rituals. This is precisely why I host every one of my retreats in a sacred space.

We are energetic beings, after all. If you go to a spot notorious for partying, you'll battle with this energy your entire stay and cannot be surprised when people are up late socializing and making noise.

If a particular location you choose is known for healing, you cannot help but absorb some of these healing vibrations. If you choose to retreat in a location where people over time have gathered with great intentions for their inner life, you can tap into their legacy to shift your mindset. These vibrations and legacies are subtle, but they can only help you.

Schedule

Creating a consistent schedule to follow while on a solo retreat is essential. It might feel nice to just let the days come and go as they will. But that is not a retreat; rather, it is a personal vacation.

On a retreat, you need a container within which you can settle into new habits, routines, and rituals to bring about the most awakening. This way, you don't become lazy or overactive. You break from the routine and pace of daily life back home once you enter into your new schedule, but you don't just fritter the day away following your every carnal impulse.

Again, a retreat has higher spiritual intent. So you must create a new normal that you can follow and stick to for the duration of your time away. No matter what kind of retreat you take, I suggest several sitting meditations per day. If you're a beginner, I recommend ten to twenty minutes per session. Practitioners with more experience can welcome twenty- to sixty-minute sessions. Optimally, aim for three to four sessions per day.

While some religious traditions emphasize meditation, meditation is a practice in healthy psychology that doesn't have to carry any particular religious affiliation. Adding meditation to your schedule is essential for both energetic shift and healthy psychology while on retreat. Not to mention it creates fertile ground for numerous personal breakthroughs.

Duration

Any length of retreat has benefits, even one day. And this decision may be partially made for you given your life circumstances. However, when making the decision for how long you can get away for retreat, be careful to avoid being seduced by the limitations of your daily calendar.

When we are in the midst of the pace we regularly uphold, it feels impossible to pull away for more than a weekend. *How could I leave the kids? I can't take time off work! My partner would never be supportive!* we say to ourselves on repeat.

There are many ways that the egoic, *little me*, old self wants to keep you in your box of comfort. From years of both practicing and hosting retreats, I can say with complete confidence that once you are actually *on* retreat, it always goes by too quickly. Participants always wish they'd had more time on their retreat and can't believe how concerned they were about leaving.

Many yoga retreats are held for a week because of the resort requirements, while traditional Vipassana retreats are ten days long. My suggestion is at least a week if you can swing it. It takes at least a day or two to drop the frequencies we came in carrying from home. While a weekend retreat can be a nice reset, a week or ten days can be completely transformative. And you can only imagine what a month could do.

Be gracious with yourself when choosing for how long you'll retreat. Our lives go by so quickly and punctuating them with intervals of retreat can slow them down and create beautiful resets. Rest assured, you'll know once you're on retreat that it was all worth it and find yourself wishing you had more time.

Logistics and Supplies

When planning your own retreat, it's important to plan for everything you'll need during your time away so you don't have to worry about it on your actual retreat. Will you be cooking your own food? What utensils, groceries, and supplies will you need? Do you need to bring your own yoga mat, meditation cushion, and sleeping bag? How will you travel to your location? Is there someone on-site to help you if you need it? What about in case of an emergency? Do you need certain books and audio recordings? Is there potable water? Hot water? Towels?

You'll want to consider all these details before booking a site for retreat. Again, you don't want to spend retreat time on trivial details that could be spent in many other valuable ways.

Certainly, there are advantages and disadvantages to retreating on your own. Depending on your intention, desired outcomes, and budget, a solo retreat might be just what you've been seeking. For more guidance on solo retreats, subscribe to my Insider Tribe at www.briedoyle.com.

ORGANIZED RETREATS

Organized retreats can be an excellent choice, particularly if you've never retreated before. Even if you've retreated for years, opening yourself up to new ideas, systems, and practices can flush new energy into your already strong practice of retreat. Furthermore, if you live alone or tend to spend a great deal of time alone, joining a group can be a wonderful way to change your pattern and welcome new inspiration into your life.

Without a doubt, the most important factor when considering joining an organized retreat is the host or teacher. If you plan to stay at a group facility but run your own retreat, like a monastery, *vihāra*, temple, or church, the guide is not nearly as important. But if you plan to participate in a structured retreat of any form, the guide can make or break your experience.

Knowing your guide personally is not essential. However, familiarizing yourself with him or her before your weekend-, week-, or monthlong retreat is a wise step on your path to self-discovery.

Any skilled guide should offer opportunities for you to get to know your instructor's style style. This may come in the form of regular newsletters or blog content, social media, or even a scheduled call to answer questions you might have about your upcoming retreat. Testimonials on the web are another great way to evaluate your guide's credibility and capacity to create a retreat that offers what you're after.

Even if you know your guide, I suggest reaching out to her and asking a few essential questions to make sure your intentions are aligned. It would be unfortunate to create the space for yourself to pull away from life back home only to get to your retreat and realize her personality, worldview, or retreat plans are not at all what you need or want.

Below is a suggested list of questions to ask your guide prior to retreat. You may have some of your own to add to this list too. Email or schedule a phone call. Even if the teacher themselves cannot answer these questions for you, someone on their team should absolutely be able to. You want to go into your retreat feeling confident that your experience will be worthwhile and that your guide is the right person to take you through this journey.

Questions to Ask Your Retreat Guide

1. What does our daily schedule look like?
2. Is there a theme to your retreat? What content do you offer?
3. Do we have free time each day? For how long?

---

4. What is your background? Credentials? Experience? Specialties?
5. What makes your retreats unique? Special?
6. What are the outcomes for your participants?
7. Who is your typical client? Who is this retreat right for?
8. What is the most common feedback you receive from participants?
9. Do you have any repeat clients?
10. Do you help with travel logistics, or do I do that myself?
11. What kind of communication can I expect from you before the retreat?
12. Can you put me in touch with a past participant?

Hearing responses to these questions will give you a great feel for what you're about to experience, as well as give you a sense of who your guide really is and what kind of program they've designed.

Attending with Friends

Many people like to attend organized retreats as a couple or with a group of friends. This can be a wonderful experience in intimacy and friendship if you bring the right person/people. It can also be an unfortunate missed opportunity to connect with yourself if you and your buddy do not have some shared understandings.

As I've discussed before, some people come on retreat just to have fun and have a new experience. This is a beautiful intention. But so much more is possible. While it may sound at first appealing to get a big group of friends together to share this experience, again, this falls more into the category of vacation than retreat. I suggest being more selective if you do choose to bring other people along on your retreat journey.

Any organized retreat should be set up to accommodate solo participants. So do not fear coming alone. Being alone on an organized retreat really allows for the best of both worlds—plenty of connection with newly formed acquaintances as well as solo time.

If you do come with a partner or friend, be sure to have a discussion prior to your journey about what you envision your time to be like together. I strongly suggest allowing time for silence in the mornings or at some point in your days, even if you share a room. This honors the need to hear your own thoughts more loudly than the thoughts of each other. Intimacy with your partner or friend is a wonderful outcome but is a secondary intention for a retreat.

With our friends and partners, we can so easily bring the patterns of relating to each other on our retreat with us. We can use them as a crutch to avoid going deeper into ourselves. Or we can quickly make having fun the only focus when so much more depth is available.

The goal is to flow into a new paradigm and allow our old patterns to drop to the background so we make way for our own creative insights and breakthroughs. A connection from home may keep us tied to the preretreat version of ourselves—unless we have these critical conversations.

If you're considering bringing a friend or partner, below are questions you can answer together in order to align your visions for your retreat and ensure you each, individually, get the most value.

Aligning with Your Partner Prior to Retreat

1. What is your intention for retreat?
2. How much alone time do you need?
3. Do you want any time for silence?
4. How should we schedule alone time and silence into our days? Mornings? Afternoons? Meals?
5. Do you want to meet new people or mostly stick with me?
6. How should we handle any conflict that comes up?
7. What else do you need from me to best support you?
8. Is there anything else I should know?

There are countless ways to retreat. Whether you choose to go it alone or join an organized retreat, there is great benefit for you. Explore the checklist below to help you better understand what you want at this point in time.

I suggest answering these questions *every* time you take a retreat. We are all constantly shifting and evolving, and as a result, our needs and desires are too.

Add up the columns to see which one has more checks. This will help you determine which type of retreat is right for you right

---

Solo or Organized Retreat?

For each line, using one from each column, repeat the following phrase:

I desire more of this (Self-Guided Retreat column) or that (Organized Retreat column).

Then check the box in the column that best describes what you want/need *right now.*

Self-Guided Retreat	*Organized Retreat*
☐ Quiet time	☐ Stimulation and conversation
☐ Meditation and or prayer	☐ Inspiration and new ideas
☐ Free time	☐ Guidance
☐ Fluidity of schedule	☐ Structure in schedule
☐ Introspection	☐ Connection
☐ Unstructured learning	☐ Organized programming
☐ Ability to plan logistics (food, travel details, etc.)	☐ Freedom from logistics to plan/prepare (food, travel details, etc.)
☐ Self-discipline	☐ External framework and follow-up

now. If you're about even in both columns, sit on it for a few days. Ask yourself before you go to bed one night, *Which type of retreat do I desire now, solo or organized?*

Let your subconscious mind chew on it. See what you wake up feeling. There's no wrong answer. You're merely seeking what would be most supportive for you at this point in time.

Chapter 12

THE ELEMENTS
OF RETREAT

The moon
abiding in the midst
of serene mind;
billows break
into light.[1]

—Dogen

Now that you've made the decision whether to join a group or create a retreat of your own, let's look at key Elements that should be a part of every retreat.

Using these Elements as your guide, you should be able to create the retreat you desire. If you plan to join an organized retreat, using these Elements will help you form good questions to ask the host to make sure your needs are met while on retreat.

SOLITUDE

I suggest a healthy portion of solitude for some part of your retreat. Even if you have a roommate or are on a group retreat, making space for just yourself while on retreat is essential. If you do share a room, consider trading mornings with your roommate where one leaves for a walking meditation or prayer and the other stays in the room to do meditation practice. And then switch the next day. If you are alone but have regular organized sessions, find your solitude at mealtimes, in the mornings or evenings, or between sessions.

Two of the most difficult patterns for women to break are the expectation to be social and the expectation to be a nurturer. Our ability to offer care is certainly one of our greatest gifts. But if we spend the entire retreat catering to the explicit and implicit needs of others to be pleasing and liked, we miss our opportunity.

Or if we use our every moment to socialize, we have not changed a pattern, only brought our behavior from home on retreat. We will not go home with an abundance of new insights or feeling the fullness that we seek. This is why solitude is such a critical tool while on retreat.

Solitude is not synonymous with loneliness. In fact, being comfortable alone is one of the greatest gifts we can give ourselves. Part of why we left home was to reunite with this inner knowing. And in order to fully do so, we must create some space for ourselves while on our retreat.

While we may at first resist and even struggle during times of solitude, finding comfort in ourselves is what we're after. A serene strength lies just beneath the surface of our being where so much of our truth sits. But we have to slow the pace and allow for solitude to find it.

Disconnect from Home and Work Life

I tell all my retreat participants to send one final email to loved ones and work (if necessary) letting them know that you are safe and happy but will be out of touch for the duration of your retreat. It may at first be tempting to send regular updates or check in with family. Especially if you have young children at home, aging parents, or pressing work matters. But this undermines the point of retreat.

The purpose of retreat is to disconnect from your life to find what is within you for yourself and to share with those you love once you return. Setting firm boundaries with your close ties back home allows you to focus on yourself. Sending an email as a gentle reminder when you begin your retreat or having a conversation with your loved ones at home prior to leaving sets you up for the greatest retreat success.

Not only does this boundary help your loved ones understand your needs; it reminds you of your intention. During moments when you're feeling lost or low on your retreat, which will inevitably happen, you may yearn for the comfort of close connections. But during these moments of challenge, choosing to stay with yourself instead of filling this discomfort with the distraction of another leads to the most self-discovery.

If you run to something outside yourself to find comfort in your low moments, you will miss your opportunity to build your own inner reserves. It is this strength that you want to bring back home to put into use when you hit a challenging moment in your day-to-day life. This is how you build your emotional muscle. You stay with yourself when it's uncomfortable or boring. And this is why setting some kind of boundary upfront around communication is essential.

One of the great outcomes of retreat is that you realize how capable the rest of your family or team is. You may unintentionally be enabling unwanted behaviors at home or work, and your retreat exposes this. You learn your children are just fine while you are away. Your partner can take great care of matters at home, and your work will get done in due time.

I am always amazed when I come home from my own retreats to see that my children are doing things on their own that I often do for them, and my husband can handle way more than I let him do daily. It reminds me to keep a close eye on how I permit my circumstances to depend far too much on me, which perpetuates my burnout.

When I come home refreshed, I am more willing to let others in my family take charge of what they can easily do on their own. I can step back and relax, remembering that my job is not to do everything for everyone around me. I don't want to create entitled kids or an uneven partnership, so my stepping back is essential. Both for me and for them.

Furthermore, there is nothing like distance to spark the flame in your intimate partnership and remind you of what you already have in front of you. By the end of your retreat, you'll feel elated to go home, see your people, and jump back into your life. And your partner cannot be more excited for your return.

They realize how much you offer after having to do everything by themselves without you. Your children grow more confident and independent. And you bring a new surge of energy to your relationships, your work, and your mission upon your return.

This respected distance allows for gratitude to rush in once you are home. But only if you hold to your boundaries of staying reasonably disconnected.

RECONNECT TO BASIC NEEDS

The first, most essential step on your retreat is to take care of yourself. It sounds so obvious but in practice can be so difficult. You may be in a hurry to plug right into the flow of the group you've joined or take on every new practice that's suggested at your retreat site. We are used to doing things well at home, and we want to carry this over into our retreat.

But first, you check in with your basic physical needs.

Begin by prioritizing sleep, nourishing food, comfort in your surroundings, reconnection with nature, and ample downtime above all else for the first day or two of retreat. Many participants come into their experience completely wound up, as if they raced to the finish line to make it to retreat. I certainly know this feeling too. However, once you arrive, you can start to slow it down by handling your primal needs first.

This means if there is a morning meditation, prayer, or yoga class you really want to go to but you are exhausted from sleep deprivation, you miss the class. This means that if you often skip showers at home because you're taking care of everyone else in your family, you take daily showers. It means that if normally you check in with work first thing each day, you leave your computer off and go for a walk in the woods or on the beach. It means that before you participate in anything at all at the retreat center, you handle your own needs first.

This advice may, at first, sound silly. *Of course I take care of myself*, we think. But many of us are living lives that drain us little by little, where not a crack of spaciousness exists. Whether it's because you're doing too much, not eating nourishing meals, not sleeping enough, or haven't seen the sun set for months, these habits will unravel you slowly over a lifetime.

On retreat, bathe yourself in healthy habits to begin to build the most updated, healthy, and aligned version of yourself. Bring attention to your basic physical needs being beautifully met first. Safety, food, sleep, hygiene, spending time in the natural world, proper downtime—these are the primary needs to dial in before plugging in to any external schedule. Only then can you dig into your next level of mental, emotional, and spiritual needs.

Until then, first things first.

Check In with *These* Basic Needs

1. *Safety and comfort*—We need the following: clean and comfortable sleeping arrangements, access to help if needed, warm or cold enough temperatures, clean water, access to food, and safe and sanitary shower and bathing options.
2. *Nourishment*—Our bodies need different types of nourishment at different times in our lives. Determine whether you need light and fresh meals, warm and comforting meals, or something else entirely. Be intentional about the food and drink you consume while retreating. Let your selections serve your greater retreat intention.
3. *Sleep*—Allow your body to naturally fall asleep and wake when it needs to, at least for the first two days. Allow for naps during the day. Retreat is a chance to rewire your circadian rhythm.
4. *Hygiene*—Take regular showers or baths, and keep yourself, your space, and your things tidy. This allows for our inner world to also feel light and at ease as well as foster a deep sense of care for yourself. Avoid toxic cosmetic products during this time. Allow your body to be natural, and avoid any product or routine that would prevent toxins to release through the skin, hair, breath, fecal, or urine channels.

5. *Movement in nature*—Our ancestors knew the importance of connecting with nature. Putting our face
toward the sun and our feet on the ground biochem-
ically influences our mood and our sense of connection to the greater world. Witnessing patterns in
nature reminds us to emulate them in ourselves. A
slowly opening bud reminds us there is a ripe time
for everything. A tree reminds us to stay rooted, take
up space, and stand tall. Seeing the sun set inspires
awe and wonder in our hearts. Nature offers powerful
symbols for us at every turn. On retreat, make time to
move your body each day in the natural world.

6. *Proper downtime*—Build in time for rest. Just as you
allow yourself to be active, balance this out by holding
space for naps, massages, reading, journaling, meditation, and quiet solo reflection. Even if your program
doesn't offer downtime, build it in yourself.

EXPANSIVE SELF-STUDY (MENTAL AND EMOTIONAL)

Now that your basic survival needs are met, you can take your
self-care to the next level. For every retreat I host, I suggest participants bring at least two personal growth, spiritual, or religious books to read during their downtime along with a journal.
I also suggest choosing podcasts or inspiring audio teachings to
alternate with reading. Sometimes we grow tired of reading, and
audiobooks offer a nice alternative.

I believe that the media we consume influences us greatly,
particularly when on retreat. When on retreat, you are a wide-
open field, ready to welcome a flowering of new ideas. When
you have time to read and reflect, choosing material that will
uplift and stimulate you allows for the greatest insights, awakening, and inspiration.

Doing the research prior to your retreat to find books and
podcasts that will inspire you is well worth your time. To get a
list of some of my favorite and most inspiring reads delivered

right to your in-box, subscribe to my Insider Tribe on my website: www.briedoyle.com.

Depending on your retreat, you may have curriculum already determined for you. There may be a theme in place, spiritual or religious study, a daily physical practice, or content that is offered as part of your program. This can be a benefit of joining an organized retreat if you find one that is a great fit for you. When interviewing your guide, do make sure that you understand the depth of content that will be covered while on your retreat. You want to make sure your needs align with the course content on the program.

Whether you're on an organized retreat or not, having supplemental media of your own choosing will offer more personalized insights and only bolster your transformation.

HEALTHY INTROSPECTIVE PRACTICES (PHYSICAL)

The habits you hold on retreat are perhaps the most important steps to allow for inspiration and breakthroughs. In order to fully break away from your physical, mental, and emotional patterns from home and learn new things about yourself and your world, you need to create new, supportive patterns while on your retreat.

This is not to suggest that all of your patterns back home are unhealthy or unsupportive. But when you interrupt patterns, healthy or not, great learning comes. A retreat, itself, is a pattern interruption. You are staying in a new place, eating different food, and spending your days differently.

I love the analogy of a glass of water with dirt sitting in the bottom to represent our inner lives. For the time being, we can see clearly through the glass as the mud rests on the bottom.

When we start a new retreat, we stir the glass (interrupt the pattern) so the water becomes filled with mud and we cannot see through the glass anymore. The water is murky, dark, and hard to see through. Many ideas and discomforts are thrown our way, and we feel disoriented and harbor a sense of groundlessness.

But through stillness and our new practices, the mud will again settle. We will see through the glass once again. Yet this time, the pebbles and clusters of mud will resettle in a more intentional and updated way. One that we're more aware of and involved in, as opposed to patterns that were put into place for us—consciously or not.

So this is why you interrupt a pattern. To stir things up, shake them around, and see what new insights come as a result. Decide what habits, ideas, relationships, and behaviors you'd like to keep and which ones need to change. Then surround yourself with supportive habits. Below are some of the healthy, introspective practices I encourage daily on my retreats. See if any of them work for you. Add your own as well.

Healthy Introspective Practices

- yoga
- meditation or prayer
- breath work
- hikes or nature walks
- journaling
- dance
- singing or chanting
- art—paint, jewelry, draw, mandala creation, and so on
- masturbation
- self-affirmations
- ceremonies and rituals

The idea here is that you choose practices that don't necessarily have an outcome or goal in mind but feel good in the body and stimulate creative flow and the opening of energy. If growth is what you're after, I suggest starting with the items on this list you *least* want to do. This will ensure the most self-expansion.

As we discussed in the energy chapter, when we are open, profound insights of all kinds make their way to us. Furthermore, when we're not focused on an outcome, we can tap back in to just enjoying ourselves and our creations, like a child. This playful spirit allows for an elevation in mood and literally shifts our frequency and therefore what we give off in the world. This allows for the same vibration of energy to be drawn back to us, as like energies are drawn to one another.

Moving your body creates a rejuvenated flow of energy inside of you. So many of us spend a lot of time sitting for work on a typical day. Having daily practices of movement—dance, yoga, hiking, breath work, or more—allows for the flush of fluid to circulate into the recesses of your body where blood, fluid, and breath sit stagnant, waiting to be circulated.

When you move, particularly in new and unfamiliar ways, you become like that glass of muddied water. At first, it may feel foreign and uncomfortable in the body. But then our mud will settle, and we'll have an entirely new stacking of consciousness and energy.

Make sure you move every day, especially if you're sitting in multiple sessions of meditation or reading regularly. You may or may not want to do art or chanting or dancing every day, but the point is to be open to creative flow.

Choose which practices to use daily and which ones to plug in on occasion, and build your schedule around them. Your habits have the ability to shape who you are in the world. And retreating is the perfect time to experiment with new and supportive habits to help you build the best version of yourself.

MEDITATION

Meditation is its own element of retreat because it is such an essential practice to create spaciousness in your inner world. It helps you detach from the physical, external world and brings your focus inward. Meditation is how you create mental stability; it cultivates your relationship with your intuition and helps condition you to connect to your divine nature.

When you meditate, you witness your thoughts come and go, and you learn to not attach so strongly to them. This allows you to experience firsthand that you are not your thoughts or emotions. Rather, you are the observer of them.

Doing this allows you to soften your gripping and resisting when something challenging comes up in your life. You recognize your identity lies behind the initial response and is more stable than a singular, transient thought or emotion.

You handle daily situations with more ease, taking comfort in the notion that what you're experiencing is like the constantly pulsating wave of the ocean. It comes, it goes, it comes again. Attaching to a particular one only creates struggle for you. This allows you to interact with a grounded sense of comfort.

Meditation cultivates this understanding. When you train yourself to sit down and stay with yourself, you remember that your spirit is in control, not your constantly shifting emotions, bodily impulses, and external circumstances.

Furthermore, the very vibration of our brains is influenced by meditation. Some frequencies allow for insight and inspiration, while others are more functional and survival based. Learning how to access these elevated states gives us a lot of creative control when it comes to having personal breakthroughs and new creative ideas.

Among others, Dr. Joe Dispenza has written a great deal about these various brain states and how to access them. Most of us spend the majority of our lives in functional brainwave states, not even tapping our full potential for insight and creative breakthrough.

When we learn to access the brain states known as *alpha* and *theta* waves, we can literally shift the course of our lives by reprogramming old beliefs, patterns, and pains that hold us back.[2]

Meditation is the practice to access these elevated states of awareness. Meditation is what brings you beyond your conscious to your subconscious mind, where this healing and reshaping is possible.

Many of our behaviors, emotional responses, triggers, and wounds are established in childhood, well before our conscious mind is even fully developed. And they stay stuck in the subconscious mind leaving us behaving and believing in ways that no longer serve us. Oftentimes, if you're challenged in adulthood by something, it's a hardwired, subconscious pattern that was set into place in your childhood.[3]

Being able to access your subconscious mind through meditation and other internal, contemplative practices while on retreat gives you the opportunity to rewrite your story that was put into place before you had a conscious choice. It allows you to take back control. A skilled retreat guide can be incredibly helpful here. But you can do it on your own too. Meditation helps you manifest the life of your dreams and have true control in the expression of your life.

Our typical life doesn't often allow for this kind of deep work. A meditation ritual solidified on retreat and then carried out in daily life help allow for these important transformations.

Meditation Tips

- Find a quiet space and a comfortable seat.
- Be mindful of your posture—sit up straight, chin tucked slightly in, the crown of your head lifted gently. Then relax your shoulders and face.
- Rest your hands easily on your knees or legs.
- Your eyes can be open or closed—closed if you're feeling highly distracted.
- Choose either form or formless meditation style.
- Commit to two weeks of the same time and duration each day—this will help form the habit.
- Do this for a minimum of ten minutes.
- When you notice your mind going down a rabbit hole, relax, label your thought "thought," and let it go. Come back to yourself.
- Be gentle with yourself—this is not a competition with anyone else or with yourself.
- Be humble—not everyone needs to know how long and that you've meditated for the day. Your actions in your daily life will show your work.
- Be disciplined—stay with it no matter what happens externally. This is a *practice*, not a *goal*.

SILENCE AND OTHER ASCETIC PRACTICES

Just as every retreat needs portions of solitude, the same holds true for silence. Some retreat programs include silence as an inherent part of the expectations and program. But for many, silence is not a cornerstone part of the experience.

I believe silence is such a valuable tool, that no matter the expectation of the program, it's worth finding time for silence. Of course, this is easy if you're on your own retreat. But if you're part of a group, you may have to look for windows or days to practice silence—as I've mentioned, first thing in the morning, during a meal or two, or in the evenings.

Maintaining silence creates an energetic opportunity for any participant. And silence is different from solitude. We can be alone but still seek conversations with new people we meet. Or alone but loud and preoccupied in our minds. In silence, we do not seek to fill our solitude with distractions like surfing the Internet. While silence and solitude go hand in hand, they are not one and the same.

We do not realize how much energy we expend just by offering a hello and a smile to a stranger as we walk down the sidewalk or interact with a store clerk. Or how much output is invested in connecting with a friend, coworker, or family member. Do these connections build light in us? Absolutely. But can too many of them over time deplete our inner reserves? Definitely. Experimenting with silence creates a rare opportunity to rebuild energy to utilize when we're back home.

But it's not just silence that can offer us these incredible insights. Any ascetic practice, or practice of withholding, gives us valuable information about ourselves. We can experiment with fasting, or limiting our meat consumption, alcohol, sugar, or dairy, to name a few. We can take a break from the internet, cell phone use, or social media. The options for withholding are endless and really dependent on the person.

If you've always wanted to experiment with intermittent fasting, for example, a retreat can be the perfect container to give it a try. If back home there is a behavior you notice yourself doing compulsively, retreating is the exact space to experiment with withholding. Then notice how your body and mind respond as a result of this shift, and take that information back home with you. *Did I feel great doing this? Did I struggle? Did I struggle at first but then feel powerful?*

The beauty of practices of withholding is they give us a surge of information and energy. Using silence as an example, imagine staying quiet for a day. Throughout your day you notice all the spaces where you would normally fill the air with words. Some of them may be necessary. Some of them may be a result of social discomfort and therefore unnecessary.

Watch your reactions and your sensations in the body, and learn from them. Withholding something allows the energy of that particular element to build. If you stay quiet, you start to feel excited about talking again.

Alternatively, you may learn that withholding something makes you feel better. You're not excited to rush back in to using it again because in taking a break from it, you feel better.

Either way, once you are done with your practice of withholding, you have more clarity on how to use that action or item to serve you and where you may have been using it in habitualized and unsupportive ways. You can now be more intentional about the words you use and how much sugar you eat, alcohol you drink, internet you use, and so on.

Below are a few suggestions of ideas to practice withholding. See if any of them resonate with you for your retreat. Add other ideas that interest you too.

Ideas for Withholding Experimentation

- words/silence
- food (fasting / intermittent fasting)
- caffeine
- sex/masturbation
- sugar
- meat or dairy
- internet use
- social media use
- television watching
- pornography
- self-deprecating language or thoughts
- harsh words or sarcasm

RESISTANCE AS TEACHER

One of the most helpful ways to think about retreat is that your time away offers you information to take back home. Retreating allows you to observe your behaviors, your patterns, your environments, and your thinking. With this information, you can choose to

1. keep things the same;
2. substitute a new identified behavior, pattern, or thought in its place; or
3. dismiss it entirely and allow for something new to manifest.

Take notes and look for evidence throughout your retreat experience. And draw conclusions to bring home based on what you find.

Remember that resistance while on retreat is your greatest teacher. Scientists of your own life, instead of running away screaming from your discomfort or filling it with another distraction, you can ask yourself,

- *What in me is feeling discomfort?*
- *What part of me is feeling triggered, and why?*
- *What does this say about me?*
- *Do I do this same thing back home?* and
- *Do I wish to stay this way or make a change?*

Your triggered moments are how you find some of the greatest takeaways from your retreat. On one retreat I hosted, I had a client tell me for the *day of silence* that because I didn't ask her to avoid the internet, she just spent her entire day surfing the web. She was silent but distracted. She told the group that she didn't think the *day of silence* was worth it because she already spends so much of her days in silence.

After our group session, she and I had a private talk where she uncovered that surfing the web was her coping mechanism back home. She lived alone and didn't want to be single anymore. She often avoided her feelings of discomfort by engaging in copious consumption of online media and shopping. So it was no surprise that this habit showed up for her on retreat too.

Furthermore, we dug into her relationship with her own power. She had been waiting for some outside source of authority to tell her that she couldn't scan the web. Because I didn't explicitly say it, she spent her day doing it.

But why did she need me to say it? She knew she didn't want to waste a day online, given the many other beautiful ways she could have spent her day. She started to unpack all the places in her life where she'd given away her power to an outside source and then blamed the source for not living the life she'd wanted.

She came back to our group the next day and with complete vulnerability shared what she had uncovered. It was at first uncomfortable for her, but as she spoke, we could all see the lightness in her eyes once again. She had moved a metaphorical boulder that kept her trapped for decades. Now she could go home and question where else she might be giving her power away and recognize that in those moments, her tendency is to hide online when she could be out in the world.

It was a beautiful lesson that showed all of us that sometimes, the things we resist the most have the most to teach us.

CONNECT TO THE DIVINE

Aside from moving massive impediments that stand in the way of living your greatest life, retreating offers you the opportunity to connect to your own understanding of divinity.

Some of you read that last sentence and rolled your eyes. Some of you nod with enthusiasm. No matter where you stand on the spirituality spectrum, retreat gives you the chance to deepen your understanding and trust in yourself, the universe, and that which is beyond the five senses.

Carl Jung first uncovered the idea of *synchronicity*, or meaningful coincidence, in the 1920s. Among seekers and creatives, it's become a commonplace notion for which we spend our lives searching.

I experience synchronicities as little winks from the universe that expose me to the underlying connection and divine plan of absolutely everything. One of my very favorite things about retreat is how incredibly overt synchronicities appear constantly, for both me and participants, because we've made space to receive them.

I'll never forget my first major retreat abroad with a group of women. On the night of the full moon, I held a fire ceremony. The theme of the night was loss and letting go. So there was time set aside in our gathering to walk the beach to remember and connect with loved ones lost. Prior to our ceremony, the women didn't know the plan for the night, what time we'd meet exactly, and what we'd be doing.

When our ritual ended, one of the women found her way to me and told me that ten years ago, at the exact same time as our fire ceremony, her father passed away. She had tears in her eyes and couldn't believe the connection of it all. Neither could I.

This is not a unique experience on retreat. Being so open and undistracted while retreating, you cannot help but notice the connections between people, places, and events at every turn. It's as if, because you're so open, you can finally see with clear eyes what's been in front of you all along.

Experiencing so much synchronicity on retreat reminds you that it's there in your everyday life too. You train yourself to see interconnectedness and energy at work when you're in the container of your retreat, so you can come home and remember there is magic everywhere. If you can just remember to see it.

You get better at noticing synchronicities when you practice asking for signs from your source, God, or the universe. Whether you ask in prayer or in passing is not important. What's important is that you ask. For in the asking, you recognize there is something bigger than just *little me*. And it feels good to live with this sense of awe and wonder, beyond just yourself.

Ask, then open yourself up to receive answers. Because you're hyperaware of yourself, your reactions, and your surroundings on retreat, you're more apt to notice these connections. If you struggle to see connections and signs, just relax. They will come when you stop trying to find them. Release the effort and just enjoy your time, and stay consistent with your supportive habits. This is your only job. When you move from striving to receiving, your whole world opens up.

Signs come in the form of dreams or visions, connections with people, or gut feelings. They come in the midst of prayers or meditations or during movement, ceremonies, journaling, or art.

This is why it's so important to have an array of modalities to work with on retreat. Anything that stirs the mud and creates cracks for the light of divine whispers to sneak in. Use the full spectrum of the gifts you've been given—your mind, your emotions, your body, your spirit—and you allow yourself to be a vessel for communication from the divine.

Even an absence of a clear sign is itself a sign. Perhaps you need to ask a different question, try again, or open yourself up to something more obvious. Retreat reminds us to frame every moment, interaction, and manifestation as sacred. This is a beautiful gift to return home with: your enlightened frame and greater trust in your creator, the universe, and yourself—that it all has meaning.

And then, no matter what you receive, feel grateful. Say, "Thank you, God; thank you, universe," each time you recognize a sign or understand something to a new degree. Say thank you because it is a delight and a privilege to be a human in this body with this mind and spirit right now.

Get good at asking for guidance; get good at receiving answers and saying thank you. And do it over and over again. The more you do it, the more you see it. Because that which you focus on grows, and that which you are thankful for multiplies.

This is how you use retreat to remind yourself that there is wonder in the world just waiting for you to open up to it. And this is how retreat trains you to see the sacred in your everyday life again.

Chapter 13

WHAT DOES (YOUR NAME HERE) WANT?

The image of the Goddess inspires women to see ourselves as divine, our bodies as sacred, the changing phases of our lives as holy, our aggression as healthy, our anger as purifying, and our power to nurture and create, but also to limit and destroy when necessary, as the very force that sustains all life. Through the Goddess we can discover our strength, enlighten our minds, own our bodies, and celebrate our emotions. We can move beyond narrow, constricting roles and become whole.

—Starhawk, *The Spiral Dance: A Rebirth of the Ancient Religion of the Goddess*

After taking the overnight flight to get to my retreat site in Costa Rica, I was exhausted. On my third full day of retreat, having spent the first two finally catching up on all those years of early baby sleep deprivation with three small kids back home, I planned to actually leave my room for something other than meals. I wanted to make it to the pool. A lofty goal.

It was winter in Colorado, where I left; I barely made it out on my flight because of the snow. So sitting in the sun felt like a complete luxury.

I threw on my bikini and ambivalently brought my pasty, post-baby body and book up to the pool to catch some rays. I sat down in a relaxing, cushy, orange chair and closed my eyes as the sun hit my face. Ahhhhh. *This is the life*, I thought to myself. Before I knew it, I was asleep.

"Excuse me, miss?" I wasn't sure if I was dreaming or if someone was actually talking to me. "Excuse me?" I woke up, startled. I looked up to see a young and stubble-faced surf instructor standing between me and the sunshine, smiling down at me.

"Hey," he offered once I finally sat up, "you're new here, aren't you?" I nodded. "Have you been to Costa Rica before?" I shook my head, still not saying a word.

No part of me had invited conversation. I was asleep when he found me. "You should come and take a surfing lesson!" He seemed kind and was clearly excited about what he did and wanted to share his skills with the world. That is wonderful. But I was not up for it. I was literally asleep two seconds before.

"You know, I think I am just going to relax. Thanks for the offer, though." He looked at me, unconvinced. He pushed on.

"You'd have so much fun! You should really come and try! It's dreamy out there. I have an opening at a quarter to five this evening!" I thought about it. I knew I did not want to surf. I wanted to sleep, read books, journal, and meditate. But I appreciated his enthusiasm. He was trying hard.

"All right. Sure," I said weakly, "sign me up." He walked away excited, and I slumped into my lawn chair already feeling the regret in my body.

Damn, I thought to myself, *I knew I didn't want to do that. What the hell was I thinking?! Here I am in another country trying to please someone I don't even know! Ack! And why?!?*

I dragged myself off the chair and marched over to him before he left. "Forgive me," I said. "I spoke too quickly. I don't want to surf. I really just want to relax."

He looked at me shocked. I was lame and unadventurous. I lacked enthusiasm when I was in the perfect place to surf. But all I wanted was to do nothing. Not move a single muscle. *That*, to me, was the ultimate goal.

"Suit yourself," he said to me in surfer dude fashion. But I felt freaking ecstatic. I had more energy in that moment than I'd had all day. All because I picked myself over pleasing another.

○ ○ ○

Part of our insatiable need to please is coded in our physiology from our ancient, mammalian brains. Our inner cavewoman has us continually working to be pleasing, as we've discussed. Years ago, we did this in order to ensure our safety, and we still fall into this pattern today.

We continue to be pleasant to bosses who treat us like crap. We are welcoming to women who socially exclude us on the regular. We say yes to complete strangers when we really mean no. We give more than we have because we want to be liked. All these behaviors come from our ancient, animalistic need to be safe.

Being on retreat allows you the opportunity to get in touch with your human spirit as opposed to living from your human animal.[1] Instead of impulsively pleasing to be safe, you can penetrate deeper levels of the psyche and spirit by retraining this part of yourself. This work alone is enough to transform your relationship with yourself and your environment back home.

Once you've established your needs, routines, and rituals, you can begin to ask yourself with regularity, *What does (your name here) want?* Do this with unwavering frequency every time you have a decision to make on your retreat.

The very first night of the retreats I host, I have women say aloud,

What does X want?
What does X want?
What does X want?
What does X want?
What does X want?

They substitute in their own names, and they get very used to asking this question at all points on my retreats.

This exercise is inspired by my surfer-dude episode. I want to allow participants space to reprogram themselves and to make choices that are best for them at every given moment. Even if it goes against the group. Doing this takes repetition, particularly if we've grown accustomed to being an overpleaser at home.

Our default as women is to do what's expected of us, go along with the group, take care of other's needs first. It takes conscious effort to relearn how to listen to our inner voice above external expectations.

Overtly asking this question, aloud at first, is one of the ways we do this. Eventually, over the course of our time together, women start asking this question internally at every junction. And then we learn to listen to ourselves again.

But because of our conditioning, it can be hard to hear ourselves and discover what we really want. We spend a lifetime training ourselves to avoid conflict in order to stay in the pleasing zone. Perhaps not in situations where we already feel safe, but certainly in those where our sense of safety fluctuates. Too many women end up in a career they don't want or waking up next to a partner they no longer love, and they wonder how they got so far off course.

It's because they stopped listening to themselves. They've literally forgotten how. Little by little, they've stuffed their voice of knowing down further and further until it's so deep down there, it's hard to hear the whispers of the spirit. We've grown so comfortable listening to all the external pressures—I *should* be married, I *should* be a lawyer, I *should* live close to my parents, and so on—that we've completely disassociated from ourselves.

Without a doubt, this kind of personal disenfranchisement will lead to depression, loneliness, energetic depletion, the manifestation of physical health problems, and even breakdown until we find that voice again.

So on retreat, start with the small, less-threatening decisions to bring that little voice back to the surface. Being indecisive is one of the most common ways we give away our power. So even surrounding seemingly trivial matters, ask yourself, *What does X want?* Don't allow for indecision; make decisions even if you feel slightly unclear or apathetic. This is how you retrain yourself and take full responsibility for your life.

There's a yoga class at eight tomorrow. *What does X want?* And then you decide. Another woman on retreat asks if you'd like to walk the beach tonight after group session. *What does X want?* They're serving salad or pasta for lunch today. *What does X want?*

Speak to yourself in third person because the subtle shift in perspective offers the chance to clear your emotional fog and see past your biases. Once again, a pattern interruption allows you to see with fresh perspective. Referring to yourself in the third person gives you the view of the outsider looking in, one who can make decisions for X from a place of love and nurturance. In the same way that you so effortlessly take care of others.

Of course, the listening is just as important as the asking. If you ask a great question but have trained yourself away from receiving the answer, you won't realize the transformation you seek.

So you need to practice how to listen again too. Your body always has the answer if you tune in. This is part of why your meditation practice is so essential on retreat. Get comfortable with being quiet and noticing subtlety in yourself and your environments.

One of the best ways I teach my clients to know their true desires is to use breath as their body guide. Let's say some of the women want to get drinks at night after we've finished with our ceremony. "Sandra" is trying to decide whether to join the group or go back to her room, read, and journal for the night. The bar sounds fun, and she really does love some of the other participants on this retreat. But she usually sleeps better if she doesn't drink, and she hasn't had a chance to journal yet today.

So she asks herself the question about going to the bar: *What does Sandra want?* If she notices herself inhale after asking the question, the answer is yes, she should go to the bar. If she notices herself exhale, the answer is no, she should go back to her room. The body doesn't lie. And breath is the perfect guide to help us see this.

Inhaling is an act of welcoming and receiving energy and air. The body sits up tall, the eyes open wider and gaze upwardly, the chest and lungs expand, and the edges of the mouth turn up in a subtle grin. This is the action of *yes*. *Yes*, I have it in me. *Yes*, I have space in me to bring in more. *Yes*, I want to receive and welcome this opportunity.

Exhaling is the action of releasing, letting go, pushing air away from the body. The body slightly drops down, the lungs contract, the eyelids droop, and the gaze sinks. This is the action of *no*. *No, I push the notion of this idea away from me now. No, I need something else that would fill me like an inhale. And this is not it.*

Got a Decision to Make? Try This . . .

- Ask yourself in third person, *What does X want?* five times (repeating is important).
- Take three deep breaths, and keep the mind relaxed.
- Ask yourself your proposition at hand in the affirmative.
  - *Should I take this new job? Do I want to take this trip?* and so on.
- Notice if you inhale or exhale.
- Notice how your body responds—does it expand or contract?
- Process what you uncover.

This process should not be repeated back to back because then the mind gets involved. Give at least an hour before trying again.

It's a simple somatic experiment that can guide you to your truth. Notice I didn't say the *right* direction. It isn't about making the *right* decision. And this is what's so important to distinguish, particularly for women who are seeking to feel safe.

It's about learning what feels true and real for "Sandra" in that particular moment. There is nothing righter than what is true for us individually. *Right* is not external; it's internal. We need to retrain ourselves in these subtle ways to find our own *right*, as opposed to the *right* of others, or we will always be depleted.

Giving yourself the chance to make small decisions allows confidence, certainty, and trust in yourself when making the bigger ones. This is why you practice asking what you want with even the smallest decisions on retreat. You fuel yourself for when you have to make the more significant choices back home. It's how you take back your power and live from your sense of spirit as opposed to just reacting out of your inner cavewoman.

So the question is, What do *you* want next?

Chapter 14

LAWS FOR RULE BREAKERS

I pray for the courage
To walk naked
At any age
To wear red and purple,
To be unladylike
Inappropriate
Scandalous and incorrect
To the very end.

—Gloria Steinem, *Moving beyond Words: Age, Rage,*
Sex, Power, Money, Muscles; Breaking Boundaries of Gender

Keeping in mind the invitation in part 1 of the book to "be bad," or challenge conventions that do not work for you, I'd like to offer some structure to use when building your own retreat. If you host retreats, these schedules will offer guidance that will nurture your participants while including all of the Elements of Retreat. If you're joining an already-organized program, you can compare your retreat flow with the schedule offered here and decide what adjustments you'd like to initiate to make your retreat your own.

There is no teacher, retreat guide, guru, or religious figure who knows more about what you need at a given moment than you do. If you're really going to live your biggest life, you have to take responsibility for the details—in life and on retreat. This means pushing boundaries and breaking rules if they don't serve you.

It is easy to celebrate women who have created beautiful lives by following a trajectory that we deem worthy. Based on our conditioning of conformity, it can be difficult when we see a woman doing something out of the realm of *our* normal—being too bold, too self-assured, too independent, too self-indulgent, and so on by *our* standards.

On a recent retreat I hosted, I had a few women come who wanted to party. They wanted to do some yoga, do some surfing, and then hit the bars. The inner work we were doing was not what they sought; this was clear immediately by their intermittent participation.

I could sense the discomfort building among the rest of the group. Some partner activities became difficult because we were never sure if these women would show up or not. And when they did show up, they were missing critical pieces from prior sessions.

At first, I felt anxious because I could tell the retreat was not jiving with these women. *Little me* felt insecure and wondered if I was doing something wrong. But then I remembered what I'd opened up at the beginning of retreat: *What does X want?* As they chose the bars over nighttime ceremonial gatherings, I realized they were offering our group a living example of this initial lesson.

I heard murmurings from other participants about their agitation with these women. But I continued to frame them with honor. Because the truth was, they were doing what *they* wanted to do. Even if from our perspective, they were missing out on a transformational opportunity. Though they wanted more of a girls' party trip than a retreat, their needs were just as valid as everyone else's.

The ability to go along with what is expected of us in a given environment does not make one person more spiritual, deep, and committed and another shallow. It takes courage to break implicit or explicit rules when they do not meet your needs.

If we're really going to create a new paradigm for women that breaks the model of "all before the self," we have to celebrate women who break rules. Even when they make us uncomfortable. Especially when they make us uncomfortable. And even when we think they're wrong. Because no matter what it looks like on the exterior, their dissent is an act of listening to themselves. It is these exact women who have lessons to teach us all about courage.

That said, when considering an actual retreat, it is important to strike a balance between living from impulsive whims on the one hand and adhering to a rigid schedule on the other. If retreat, renewal, and personal inspiration are what you seek, keeping some personally chosen or agreed-upon rules in place is essential.

Being able to flex within your framework is important. However, we must learn to recognize the difference between running from discomfort because we don't like it (who does?) and sticking with it because growth is needed and the outcome will be worth it.

One thing is for sure: if at any point your safety—physical, mental, emotional, or otherwise—is threatened, this is a clear sign that you need to make a change and trust your inner voice.

In the next section, we'll talk about how the group leader, the experience, the curriculum, and so on may stir some feelings of anger, discomfort, or frustration in you during your retreat. This is a normal process of self-growth that can actually be very useful. But if this discomfort is sustained throughout your entire experience, it is not a right match, and something needs to change.

When considering your framework and involving each of the Elements of Retreat, here are a few schedules to try on for size. Keep what you like; tweak what you don't.

Retreat Sample Schedule #1

This schedule is designed for a participant on a solo retreat or at a retreat site where you run your own schedule.

- gentle morning movement (yoga, walking)
- meditation session #1
- journal writing: three pages
- breakfast
- hiking: engage the senses
- breath work to clear energy
- meditation session #2
- lunch, free time
- meditation session #3
- listen to teachings on a podcast or read

- *open time*, relax, create, nap, move, and so on
- outside time, watch the sun set if possible
- dinner
- meditation session #4
- listen to teachings or read
- final journal entry
- personal care, shower, bathe, stretch

Retreat Sample Schedule #2

This schedule is designed for a retreat host/hostess or a participant going on a group-planned retreat.

- gentle morning movement (yoga, walking)
- meditation session
- journal writing: three pages, breakfast
- group curriculum time
- lunch
- *open time*, relax, read, create, nap, move, meditate, and so on
- outside time, watch the sun set if possible, group hike or beach time, and so on
- dinner
- nighttime ceremony
- socialize or solo time to journal, meditate, read, and so on

Both schedules have all components for a healing and inspiring retreat experience. As you can see, the solo retreat offers more structure, and the group retreat assumes structure is inherent in your experience. Incorporating all the Elements of Retreat offers you the greatest chance of personal transformation. But how you schedule your days should feel nurturing and supportive to you first and foremost.

Chapter 15

DROPPING THE GURU OBSESSION

Why would even the most realized beings want people to become reliant on his wisdom instead of their own?
—Diana Alstad and Joel Krammer, *The Guru Papers*

Too often we are seduced into believing that we need something outside of ourselves to make us well. We follow the latest exercise trend, consume the latest supplements, and join popular gyms in hopes that we'll look and feel exactly how the advertisements promise.

This holds true with spirituality too. We tend to believe that we need a particular practice, specific temple, meditation circle, set of beads, or guru to help us reach enlightenment or contemplate the afterlife.

There is something enchanting about almost anything that feels different or new. And those who can explain life's big, unanswered questions to us with conviction have our undivided attention. Often, instead of just validation of our experience, we seek all our answers and our very meaning in these hierarchical relationships—yearning for something outside of ourselves in a way that is often unhealthy and self-dissociative.

When an appointed or self-ascribed leader guides with a sense of certainty, we feel at ease in our uncertainty. But there is no human being who knows what's best for another or can speak what is true for anyone else. It is tempting to play into the childish hope that something external can quell our primal fears around living and dying.

When we're conditioned to believe that some outside agency, power, or person will solve all our problems, we risk wedding ourselves entirely to that source. But the thought of dropping this belief—letting go of our reliance on an outside force—is extremely difficult and can be devastating because then we're left with only our own limitations. And this doesn't feel nearly as enchanting as believing in previously established dogma or someone else's eloquent words cloaked as truth.

But the authoritarian model is concerning and can even be dangerous. We've all heard tales of powerful gurus who exploit this kind of power—stories of sexual scandal, unprecedented financial gain and recognition—at the hands of thousands of devoted followers. Or of the countless priests who abuse young children for decades behind the comfortable and trusting curtains of unquestioned devotion.

Unfortunately, this desperate focus on the external to bring us to our own truth reveals a fundamental mistrust in ourselves and our relationship with our intuition. It creates a gap between our own lived experience, gut feelings, visions, and understandings of divinity and that which is expected or "normal" in a given spiritual circumstance.

Yet so many of us feel we need a conduit to serve as a go-between for our relationship to the divine. One of the greatest traps of the spiritual path is to follow an authoritarian model, giving away all our own power to one system or person. When we unquestioningly wed ourselves to an ideology, spiritual person, or practice, we dishonor ourselves and are robbed of our inherent, moment-to-moment wisdom.

This is not to say people can't find deep meaning and value in following a religious path or tradition or practicing under a certain teacher or lineage. More so that we must keep our wits about us, constantly evaluating our own sense of right and wrong against the larger message. And most importantly, choose ourselves when the status quo goes against our sense of truth.

Retreating aims to build this inner wisdom so no matter your external experience, your voice is aligned, heard, and ready to take action. The intention of retreat is for you to know and care for yourself based on your own experience. You need no teacher, no guru, no dogma, no fancy site or prop in order to create this kind of meaning for yourself while on retreat. This is important to keep in mind when weighing how to choose what kind of retreat you'll do.

We are often drawn to a retreat by the status of a guru, religious authority, or powerful figurehead. A certain yoga celebrity is putting on an event, and you catch wind about it on social media. Or perhaps your local synagogue or church is hosting an annual retreat to deepen religious practice and study.

This is not to say that teachers and guides cannot be helpful along the way. They certainly can. But the true role of the guide on retreat is to foster and offer opportunities for *personal* self-discovery, not indoctrination or their own self-aggrandization.

It is important to not be swept away by the status, teachings, or devotion of other participants if something in your gut does not feel right while on retreat. This is why researching your retreat and getting to know the leader or location expectations beforehand is so incredibly important. Particularly if you plan to join an organized group.

Of course, for those who retreat alone, this is of less concern. That said, we can lose ourselves trying to uphold what we believe is expected of us even if we are alone. We can spend hours doing practices that feel esoteric, reciting words that hold no meaning for us, or showing up to groups that offer us little room for personal exploration. Alternatively, we can spend our time solely relaxing. This is wonderful but is also not truly a retreat.

None of these listed practices is inherently negative or positive. What's important here is that we check in with our own inner compass along the way as opposed to conforming to a protocol because we want to be good, be liked, or do it "right."

I speak about this with passion because I know these struggles intimately. As a self-ascribed seeker from a very young age, I've always been mystified by ancient practices and by spiritual teachings that bring me deeper inside myself. Hungry for personal growth and expansion as a young woman, I spent decades each in two different organized religions trying to rest my seeking soul.

But the truth was, both times, after years of giving it everything I had, each tradition wound up feeling like a jacket that was too tight. I felt rumblings of incongruency at my core and couldn't fake it. I left one to dive into another, believing I had found the *real* answer this time. After a decade of trying, I found the same personal limitations and conflicts in this new organized path.

I am infinitely grateful for the lessons I learned and the spiritual and moral foundation I came away with as a result of these deep dives. Some of the practices of prayer and meditation I still use today. But what makes me feel the most alive is to trust my own inner guide at every moment along the way. To me, *this* is what it means to be spiritual. And I am deeply spiritual, though no longer particularly religious.

It is not always comfortable, and it is far more work than turning myself over to something that already has established leaders, practices, supposed truths, and codes of being. But there is not an organization, guru, or ideology that knows how to live to the fullest expression of me better than I do.

Of course, every person is so different. Some find salvation in organization and others in independence. There is no right answer for all. And it is not only institutions functioning with the authoritarian model that can be problematic.

The question is, *Who or what are we giving ourselves away to now?* We may be in an intimate relationship that doesn't support us on an individual level. Or perhaps we're still trying to live up to our mothers' expectations. Or maybe we martyr ourselves to the role of the mother or to our careers.

Each of these cases makes us feel like we can't even escape for retreat to begin with. *It would be out of character with who we "are,"* we so assuredly tell ourselves. We often don't realize how much we self-sacrifice and unknowingly attach to our roles, partners, parents, careers, or ideology.

No matter. Go easy on yourself. Retreating is what brings you back. Always. If at any point you realize you are lost, you have the answer: yourself. And retreating is exactly how you find yourself again.

Part III

THE INNER TRAJECTORY OF RETREAT

Chapter 16

AN INNER EXPERIENCE

The world is full of magical things, patiently waiting for our senses to grow sharper.

—W. B. Yeats, *The Countess Cathleen*

By now, you know the reason for retreating. You know why, if you want to live your most extraordinary life, you need them regularly. You know how to decide what style of retreat you want, what factors to consider when planning for one, and the Elements of Retreat to ensure that a retreat is what you're actually creating. Not just a vacation, a girl's trip, or a party.

But what actually happens internally while you're on retreat? I am incredibly excited to share this section of the book because once you read and understand it, you'll be ready for every step of retreat. Furthermore, you'll understand why you're feeling pushed in some moments and inspired in others. You'll see that it's all part of the psychology, emotion, and energy of retreat. And you'll understand how to use this energy as momentum to bring about healing, life-altering inspiration, and transformation.

Every chapter in this section represents an inner stage that you'll go through when embarking upon your retreat. Some stages are brief—a fleeting felt experience. Other stages could last a day or many more.

But you can count on experiencing all the emotional and energetic stages while you're on your retreat. Furthermore, you'll go through them in order. You can only get to *gratitude* once you've gone through *unease and apprehension.*

In this section, I'll share stories of inspiring, brave, wise, and beautiful past participants and their experiences to elucidate how each stage manifested for them, so you can normalize for yourself when that stage comes for you. While the stages may show up differently for you, you'll be able to recognize each step as an expected point on your journey and navigate your retreat with more grace as a result.

And if you're planning retreats for others, it's important to consider these stages to help you understand where your participants will be energetically and emotionally so that your coursework pays heed to their needs. Anticipating this inner arc allows you to take care of your participants and honor the whole person—physical, mental, energetic, and spiritual—and ensures a transcendent experience for them while relishing your retreat.

The inspiration for this trajectory came to me when I was on my own retreat. It was a download from the divine; something that came *through* me but wasn't *from* me. It was like I cracked a code.

It was in going through my old journals that I'd kept for twenty years of retreats that I recognized a pattern: I went through the same emotions and energy shifts every single retreat I took. It didn't matter where I was or how many times I'd retreated; it was always the same.

I couldn't keep my pen moving fast enough in my journal to capture it all. But after some fine-tuning and years of practice implementing, I know that understanding and anticipating the *Emotional and Energetic Trajectory of Retreat* offers real value, for leaders and participants alike.

But it wasn't just the recognition of this pattern of emotional and energetic stages that we all go through on retreat that was so enlightening to me. After studying this arc and building curriculum around it to best serve my participants, I noticed that these stages link up impeccably with the chakras or energetic centers in the body.

The Sanskrit word *chakra* means "wheel" or "disk." The concept of chakras first appeared in ancient Indian Vedic religious texts. These days, *chakra* is almost a household word, and the use and understanding of them have taken on new-age appeal.

But the root and true meanings behind these centers stem from ancient Indian thought. Understanding the depth of the chakras is a practice all on its own.

Put simply, there are seven main chakras in the body that start at the base of the spine and work their way up through the crown of the head. Each of the chakras contains bundles of nerves and is associated with a major organ in the body. Both fluid and energy move through these centers, so if one becomes blocked, we experience problems—energetically, physically, emotionally, and so on.

What I uncovered when building my curriculum was that each stage a person goes through on retreat is associated with the energy of a particular chakra, moving in order, starting from the base of the spine (first chakra or root chakra), and moving up.

This was an incredible breakthrough because it meant that while on retreat, we have the opportunity to literally heal or transform our psychology as it relates to these locations in the body, from the base up, just by experiencing the stages of retreat if we are aware.

Furthermore, when we are mindful of the energetic intention of each chakra (which I'll explain in chapters 17–24), we can use this knowledge to align our energy and create even more opening in that particular chakra.

For the purposes of this book, I'm interested in the psychology of the chakras as it relates to the trajectory as opposed to the physical implications, which are often explored through yoga in the West.

In the East, understanding of the chakras is much more comprehensive and far beyond just physical. Two women I *love* following who touch on this regularly in their Instagram feeds are Jayshree Vara (@jayvara.london) and Namrata Patel (@functionalnutritionistuk).

While on an actual retreat, we practice specific yoga and meditation to activate these physical locations in the body. If this interests you, there are countless books and online resources to deepen your understanding of the chakras using yoga and meditation. I love *Wheels of Life* and *Eastern Body, Western Mind*, both by Anodea Judith.

If you want to incorporate this work into your practice, I suggest finding a local or online yoga teacher you love and exploring this concept with him or her. Our chakra discussion in this book will be primarily surrounding psychological concepts of the chakras.

In each chapter in this section, you'll hear the following:

- Testimonial—a personal story from a past participant in this stage of retreat
- Explanation—what's happening mentally, emotionally, and physically in this stage of retreat
- Chakra—a description of which chakra relates to this stage and how it does so
- Energy—what becomes of your energy while going through this stage
- Antidote—what to do once you've identified you're in this stage to make the most meaning out of your experience

With this knowledge and awareness, your retreat will be transformational for you every single time. I assure you.

It is my honor to share the *Emotional and Energetic Trajectory of Retreat* with you. I hope it helps you understand yourself so you can feel even more empowered in your retreat and life back home. Let's dive in.

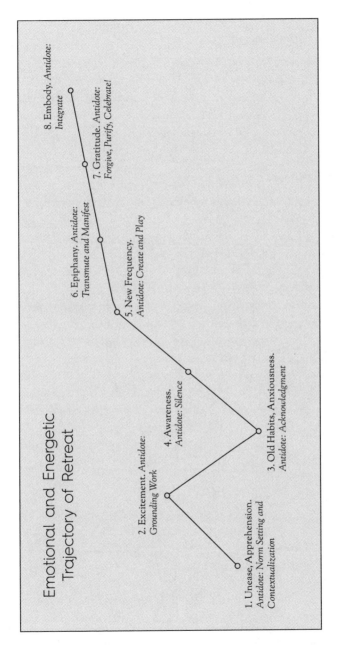

Emotional and Energetic
Trajectory of Retreat

1. Unease, Apprehension.
Antidote: Norm Setting and
Contextualization

2. Excitement. Antidote:
Grounding Work

3. Old Habits, Anxiousness.
Antidote: Acknowledgment

4. Awareness.
Antidote: Silence

5. New Frequency.
Antidote: Create and Play

6. Epiphany. Antidote:
Transmute and Manifest

7. Gratitude. Antidote:
Forgive, Purify, Celebrate!

8. Embody. Antidote:
Integrate

FIGURE 16.1

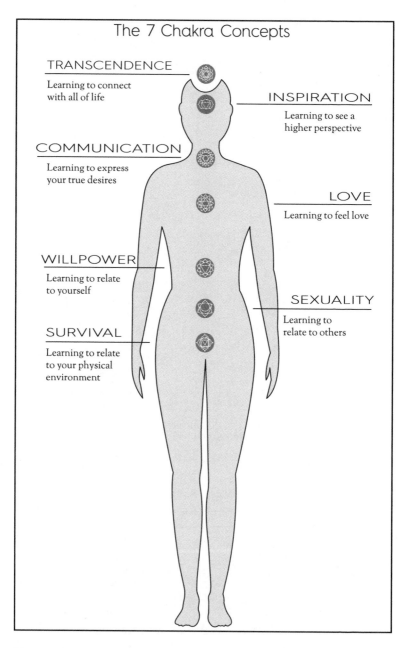

The 7 Chakra Concepts

TRANSCENDENCE
Learning to connect
with all of life

INSPIRATION
Learning to see a
higher perspective

COMMUNICATION
Learning to express
your true desires

LOVE
Learning to feel love

WILLPOWER
Learning to relate
to yourself

SEXUALITY
Learning to
relate to others

SURVIVAL
Learning to relate
to your physical
environment

FIGURE 16.2

Chapter 17

PHASE 1: UNEASE AND APPREHENSION

Affirmation: I am open to receiving. I trust what it was that called me here.

Twenty-six-year-old Maria felt nervous the moment she decided to travel all the way to the AWAKEN Retreat. She hadn't traveled abroad much but had always wanted to do more of it. Despite her fears, something in her felt called to be there.

A recent master's graduate, Maria had poured every last drop of herself into her studies for the past several years. As a result, her relationships with her peers, her partner, and herself took a backseat to her schooling.

Maria accomplished incredible professional feats as a young woman. But she started to question her identity and sense of personal wellness as her graduation ceremony approached.

Worry, depression, need for control, and stress plagued her frequently. She often felt lonely, struggled with insomnia, and overused alcohol and marijuana to soothe her stress and pull off her academic and professional workloads.

Maria knew something had to change. She wanted to find the parts of herself that went beyond academia. It had been so long since she'd accessed the creative, artistic part of herself. Had she disappeared entirely? Maria knew she was still inside. She just wasn't sure how to bring her out again.

When she saw the opportunity to go on a retreat that nourished the soul, Maria was intrigued. For much of her professional career, she'd been surrounded by men. She yearned for feminine connection. She loved the idea of getting lost in a new country, exploring her own wellness, and being held by a supportive sisterhood at AWAKEN.

Yet shortly after committing to the retreat, Maria started to second-guess her decision. Anxious thoughts overtook her psyche. *Can I really afford this trip? What will the group think of me? Do I deserve to go? What would the group think of a farm girl with dirty nails, messy hair, and a love of bugs?*

In Maria's head, she envisioned an idealized snapshot of the women in the group—prim and perfect. This made her feel even more isolated. Nevertheless and with ambivalence in her heart, she boarded the plane, open to a new experience to bring her back to herself.

Maria says of her experience,

> A rush of life captivated me as I was welcomed by an amazing group of healers. Together, we created a community and a dialogue I'd waited my entire life to be a part of.
>
> In the long run, this retreat has reshaped more than just my daily routine. My time on retreat cracked me wide open, allowing for new friendships, habits, ideas, and goals to unfold. Joy and forgiveness are now restoring a once starved space within my walls.
>
> For the first time in my adult life, I am considering the impact of my mental health on myself and others. I am taking steps to address it. I am working to build a daily practice that promotes health, esteem, and kindness. I am looking at growth as a cyclical process, not a linear one.
>
> We must return to retreat over and over again to fix damage we have incurred, just as a circle has no end. Just as I will never be done learning.

○ ○ ○

Phase 1 of retreat is *unease and apprehension.* You've made the decision to take a retreat. You've paid the money, taken the time off, and made arrangements for your family while you're away. You know how lucky you are to get this time for just yourself.

But suddenly, almost out of nowhere, you start to regret your decision. *Do I really need this? Can I really afford this or take time off? I am so busy with work, family, volunteering, and so on. Isn't it selfish for just me to go?! Besides, I've already been on a retreat before!* The list goes on and on.

For some, the sense of guilt or regret hits the moment you book the retreat. For others, it isn't until right before you leave that you start to second-guess your decision. Or perhaps something external comes up in the weeks leading up to your departure that makes the leaving feel more difficult.

Societally, retreating is not yet a normalized practice. (Though I aim to change this.) So the fact that you've chosen to retreat means you're a leader. But it isn't always easy doing what is healthy and wise before others catch on. Many people question your behavior and motive, and this exacerbates your feelings of guilt, regret, and second-guessing.

Leaving is difficult because we humans are literally chemically addicted to our states of being. For many of us, that's living with regular stress, as is so normalized in our culture.

We certainly wouldn't admit to enjoying living in stress. But stress puts us physiologically in "fight or flight" mode and releases adrenaline in the body. The experience of adrenaline is arousing and makes us feel alive. We're meant to vacillate between periods of adrenaline and stasis in the body. All animals are wired this way for survival. But with the pace of our lives today, we are living in stress constantly with very few breaks. And we grow addicted to this chemical concoction.

One of the less obvious problems with living in this state of stress is that it narrows our focus to only what is in front of us. Not only do we feel frantic and out of control; we literally cannot see beyond our duties and obligations to reorient our energy and ask, *Who have I been, and who do I want to be? Or is this working for me now?*

In fight-or-flight mode, we operate with our heads down and with excruciating focus. So much so that we miss bigger connections and meanings. We are literally unable to see how interconnected everything is and that we have both the power and the responsibility to craft our lives in a different manner. With this kind of intense focus, leaving for a different pace feels impossible. So it makes sense that we'd try to rationalize ourselves out of leaving for retreat.

Furthermore, we believe our roles to be so important in daily life that we almost can't imagine how things will exist without us there to handle everything. *My family will fall apart. My partner can't be alone. No one will do the work that needs to be done,* we fear.

But the truth is, continually living our frenzied pace and being "there to handle everything" without grounding ourselves regularly only projects more chaos into our workplaces, families, and communities.

Our resistance to leave is our attachment to our *little me,* egocentric selves. *Little me* finds significance in *what* we do: how much we accomplish at work or home, how many social gatherings we attend, how much we can volunteer or be available for others. With FOMO-like (fear of missing out) insecurity, *little me* assures us that if we step away, we'll lose part of who we are.

Our daily roles of mother, student, boss, friend, volunteer, and so on create status and identity for us, some of which are healthy. But when we are so incredibly attached to our roles that we cannot pull away to reboot, then we have fallen out of balance. We cannot be surprised when we lose our temper with our children, snap at our partner, unknowingly put on fifteen pounds, or find ourselves feeling sick all the time.

Big me knows that there is just as much value in *how* we do our lives as there is in what we do with them. But we cannot access *Big me* thinking if we're always living from *little me* conditions— running from pain to pleasure, one obligation or commitment after another.

This is precisely why *unease and apprehension* is the first stage of retreat. From your *little me* conditions of daily life, you literally can't imagine how retreating would be as important as everything going on at home. And this is where the conflict in leaving comes from.

Furthermore, when you are about to experience change, your *little me* self does everything possible to prevent it. *Little me* is all about comfort, the known experience, and living in a predictable fashion.

Though life is crazy back home, you have grown accustomed to it. To leave would be to take a risk for the unknown. There is not space in your present life for imagining what unknown connections, insights, and breakthroughs might come as a result of pulling away when operating from this pace.

And almost as if you're being tested, prior to your departure, life events surface that make you feel even more challenged to leave. Not only are you battling your inner, *little me* demons of constantly second-guessing yourself, but now you have external evidence that maybe it's not such a good idea to leave too. This is that addiction to stress beckoning you to look for manifestations in your material world to validate your reason to stay put.

Your kid gets sick right before you leave, you're given another assignment with an unrealistic deadline, a massive storm hits, and your travel is delayed. I've had folks break bones, lose jobs, get attacked by animals, and more just before they leave to join me on retreat. It's as if the universe is asking, How committed are you to this transformation of yours?

I always tell people when planning a retreat to remember *this is a time your family/workplace/partner will never remember and one you will never forget.* If you find the courage to push through the resistance to leave, you will find the transformation you've been seeking. Without a doubt. It happens every single time.

It is in the leaving that you'll know the true value of your retreat. Because there are messages that you'll only uncover if you go. It takes courage to leave that which is known for the unknown. It requires self-confidence and a greater trust in that which is beyond your known experience if you want to find more of your own magic.

So despite your reservations, you take a risk. You remember that *Big me*, visionary thinking. And trust what it was that called you to take a retreat at this very point in your life. Despite your unease and apprehension, you leave for your retreat. Congratulations, you have officially passed the first test.

CHAKRA

Because you have not yet started your retreat, we won't fully engage the conversation of the chakras until phase 2. However, at this stage of *unease and apprehension*, we're starting to evaluate the first chakra, the root chakra: *Muladhara*. Our root chakra is associated with safety and security. As you start to consider leaving the comforts of home and your known world, your very safety feels threatened in a psychological sense. The fear of change stirs something primal in you, so you begin to evaluate your connection with your root chakra.

ENERGY

As shown in figure 16.1, energy in this phase is often low. Depending on when you feel the sense of apprehension or regret, these emotions, themselves, have a lower and erratic frequency in the body and mind. So it is not uncommon to feel anxious, apprehensive, and tired one minute then excited the next as you cross through this stage.

You need only know that this is normal, and very soon your energy will build in ways you cannot even imagine.

ANTIDOTE

For this phase of *unease and apprehension*, it is important to create a new normal. The antidote for *unease and apprehension* is *norm setting and contextualization*.

When I host a retreat, I know participants have often traveled far to arrive at a new site and begin a journey about which they know very little. They may feel anxious to be a part of a new group or saddened by what they've left behind—children, work, partners, and so on. Perhaps there's just an overall unease about the unknown.

Even if you don't have these feelings of unease and whether you're joining an organized retreat or starting alone, it's incredibly important in this first phase of retreat to set some norms for yourself.

Once you arrive at your site, take out your journal and loosely jot down what you want your days to involve. You don't need to be too specific yet; just think about the big picture. Look back at the retreat sample schedules in part 2 of this book, and using them as guideposts. Start to think about how you'll build your own. Consider the Elements of Retreat and decide which ones you want to pull in for your time.

If you're on an organized retreat, hopefully the guide has some sort of welcoming ceremony, initiation, or kick-off with relevant details so you feel held at the start of your new experience. Whether you're on a solo retreat or an organized one, it's important to take the time to contextualize the experience for yourself and soak in the logistics and details.

Think about why you came, what you're there for, and what you want out of this experience. Be mindful of placing too many expectations on your retreat, but see if you can access *Big me* thinking.

Below are some suggested questions you can ask yourself to contextualize your experience in a way that will bring ease to those frequently experienced, initial feelings of unease and apprehension.

Contextualize Your Retreat

- Who am I right now, and who do I want to be?
- Why did I come on retreat at *this* point in my life?
- What do I hope to get out of this retreat?
- What is a question I want to answer during this retreat?
- How will I connect to God, the universe, source, energy, and so on during this retreat?
- During this retreat, it is most important for me to . . .
- By the end of this retreat, I want to feel . . .
- This retreat will be meaningful for me so long as I . . .

When you honor the feelings of unease and apprehension and acknowledge that you may be feeling low energy in this time by setting some norms and connecting with the bigger picture, you naturally allow your energy and emotion to rise. Doing this enables you to feel safe and purposeful and also to begin to build more authentic excitement.

Finally, if you are alone in this first phase, I'd suggest bringing in an element of ceremony to connect you to why you really came. Light a candle, take a walk at night, say a prayer, or do a meditation. This allows you to commence and celebrate your experience and make retreating a sacred practice. While the logistics are important to nail down, connecting to your spirit is really why you've come. Ceremony helps you welcome a relationship with your spirit.

If you create this connection at the very start of your retreat, you set the stage to allow your spiritual muscle to develop throughout your experience. When you begin your retreat with an element of ceremony, you open to the possibilities, insights, and deeper value that will come for you as a result of your retreat.

Once you've accomplished this, you're ready for phase 2.

Chapter 18

PHASE 2: EXCITEMENT

Affirmation: I am centered, grounded, and safe. I let go of fear. I am at peace with the material world in which I now reside.

Zadie was excited to spend a week away on retreat for herself. A busy wife and stay-at-home mom with three young boys and a husband who traveled regularly for work, she found herself desperately seeking space, personal renewal, and validation.

After a long journey Zadie arrived at the retreat center exhausted. But once she hiked up the beautiful staircase to check in, she was immediately taken with the gentle music, the tropical flowers surrounding the pool, and the sounds of jungle birds.

After morning yoga the next day, the group gathered to begin the Heart Curriculum portion of the retreat. Heart Curriculum is my signature personal growth content that's offered at retreats I host. It's researched and curated based on the theme of the particular retreat. Women mingled and began getting to know one another. Participants introduced themselves and laughter permeated the *shala*.

Immediately, everyone on the retreat fell in love with Zadie. She had an outgoing personality and a contagious laugh. Arms full of tattoos, a shaved head, and a wicked sense of humor, it was clear Zadie was bringing the fun to the group.

Though bold and fierce on the exterior, Zadie was a sensitive and intuitive soul. She felt sad and anxious to leave her boys at home, and this weighed heavily on her heart. She'd never left her younger one for longer than a few days. And she feared that taking this retreat for just herself was indulgent and maybe even selfish.

Despite her trepidation, Zadie was hungry for some kind of healing. Her father had passed away after a horrible battle with cancer just a few months prior. And she didn't have the chance to say goodbye. She carried this with her constantly. But with three young boys and such a full life, there was not much time to think about how deeply this affected her.

After dinner, participants watched a documentary that related to the content of the week. The group had a window of time to socialize while the movie and popcorn were set up.

Some women mingled; some women stuck to themselves. Zadie wanted to socialize. This group was already bonding particularly strongly. Zadie regularly had women keeled over from laughter.

A few women decided to grab a drink from the bar before the movie. And what the hell, they were having fun. One drink quickly became two.

Zadie showed up to the movie feeling in good spirits. She was a regular pot smoker and came to the retreat wanting to look at this relationship. What moments did she reach for marijuana, and why? It was a question she continued to ask herself.

It wasn't that she believed her relationship with pot was unhealthy. She just used it to relax. But she didn't want to *need* pot to calm down. Just to enjoy. Zadie wanted to experiment with cutting back while on retreat.

As the group sat down to watch the movie and Zadie's excitement continued to rise, she chewed up a THC gummy. Fully relaxed, she watched the movie then went back to her room to converse with her roommate.

Her mouth became dry, she lost her train of thought, she kept talking with her roommate. And finally, she fell asleep for the night.

The next morning at the Heart Curriculum session, Zadie shared her story with the group. Out of excitement, nervousness, and habit, she had taken it further than she meant to the night before. *Why did I eat that pot gummy?* she wondered aloud. She reached for what she did back home when big emotions or anxiousness arose without thinking about it.

This was a moment of insight.

She had recognized her pattern. More importantly, she'd seen what she does unconsciously in her home life. After this point on retreat, Zadie remembered the other tools she had used in the past that had offered her solace her entire life. Journaling, meditating, and drawing with fun markers breathed life, clarity, and calm into her in a way that marijuana did not. She remembered this being on retreat.

She says this of her experience:

Being on retreat was the perfect opportunity to reflect on *who* I am and *how* I am. Being in a group setting where most of the people didn't know me but came for similar reasons was so powerful. Putting myself in an unfamiliar yet embracing setting was an ideal time to look at my own patterns and behaviors.

The retreat impacted me in so many positive ways. It was life changing really. I have a completely different appreciation for myself and my ways. I felt like I had a year of therapy in one week. My self-esteem has turned upside down. And the gratitude I have for my family and friends is prolific. I now see that they love me no matter what, and I can finally receive this love.

O O O

You've made it through your apprehension, and you've finally arrived at your retreat site! You're here. You're actually doing this. All the planning, logistics, and effort it took to take this time off have finally come to fruition. Congratulations!

After moving through phase 1 of retreat, you will naturally enter phase 2: *excitement*. This is the beautiful high you've been waiting for. It takes a lot to pull away. Finally arriving feels like a major accomplishment. And as you start to familiarize yourself with your new setting, there will be a natural build in emotion and energy.

You realize that all your fears about leaving were unnecessary. Everyone and everything back home are fine. Perhaps you start to walk around your retreat site, or if you're part of a group, you meet people in your program, and this lifts your energy.

If you've been intentional about planning prior to retreat, now is when you start to feel really great about your decision to come. The site looks amazing, the food is delicious, the teacher seems wonderful, your opening ceremony makes you giddy; you are in a stage of outrageous openness. Everything at this phase feels euphoric.

It's important to celebrate these feelings of anticipation in this phase, and it is equally important to understand them. I liken these feelings of excitement to Christmas morning feelings for children. They are so incredibly high because you have been waiting for this moment. In some cases, for an entire year or more. And it has finally arrived.

CHAKRA

In phase 2, we begin the conversation of how our experience links to the chakras. You have now arrived into a new space, physically, mentally, and energetically. In order to ensure your sense of safety, you honor the first chakra, the root chakra: *Muladhara* in Sanskrit.

The root chakra is physically located on the first three vertebrae at the base of the spine and the coccyx. It is associated with the color red, which is the densest and most stimulating of all the colors in the chakra system. It commands your attention, like a stop sign or a red light. Paying attention to your root chakra requires this same consideration.

Conceptually, this chakra relates to your sense of safety and survival.

If you begin your retreat and do not get these basic needs right—your sense of safety and belonging—you cannot go any further within yourself on your retreat. This is why it's so important that you take care of your basic needs first if you want to experience transformation and go deeper in your experience.

First chakra questions that arise at the start of a retreat include, *Do I belong here? Am I safe? How can I relate to my physical environment?*

ENERGY

This stage brings with it a natural lift in energy. New environments and experiences have a way of triggering our sense of openness. When we have few expectations and feel safe, we feel a lift in energy at the start of a new experience.

Like Zadie's story, you are trying to navigate your feelings of excitement. You know no other way than to play out your energetic patterns of excitement from home. When you feel excited, you may drink, oversocialize, commit to too much, divert, distract, overgive, tend toward perfectionism by trying to do everything "right" on your retreat, incessantly set up your room, read through your manuals, and more.

While energy heightens in this phase, sometimes present are two dueling energies—that of excitement and anxiousness. You feel excited but insecure in who you are and how to relate to yourself in this new environment. This kind of anxious excitement is similar to the stress hormones you experience back home, so your body responds with a familiar chemical release.

The goal of retreats is to bring your anxious frequency down and allow your energy to authentically expand by penetrating the deeper parts of yourself. This takes time and being with yourself throughout the highs and lows of retreat.

The energy in this second phase is surface level, synthetic, and your false summit. You have not even scraped the surface of the depth of energy that your full retreat experience will bring you by the end. While your energy is elevated at this phase, it is erratic, draining, and unsustainable for the long term.

But this is a natural and essential phase to go through while retreating. In this phase, allow yourself to feel the full excitement, trusting that more is coming for you. The antidote teaches you to do so in a healthy manner.

ANTIDOTE

The antidote in phase 2 of retreat is *grounding work*. During this time, you need to create new roots for yourself. Because your surroundings have changed and many of your normal comforts have been stripped away, you need to create a new sense of stasis in order to get the most out of your experience and allow for an essential sense of physical, mental, and emotional safety.

Furthermore, because the energy is so synthetically high, you need to offer yourself polarity with practices of grounding to stay in balance and not hemorrhage all your energy at the start of your retreat.

There are many different practices that can be grounding while on retreat. Because this chakra has to do with connecting to your physical environment, anything that helps you do that in this phase offers value.

On retreats I host, I have my participants take a walk around the property. Or when we're in an international location, I have them go into the town and connect with locals. This helps them get their bearings and locate themselves in the greater community. And having a contact person in town gives a stronger sense of confidence when spending time in this new location.

Aside from connecting with people, being in nature is a wonderful way to ground in this stage. Nature reminds us to slow down, that everything has a divine time. Being in nature offers us countless profound lessons to start to bring us back to ourselves.

After all, everything in nature is an expression of energy, just like you are. A tree has a perfect vibration, as does the sand and the ocean. I always have my participants take their shoes off, put their feet in the sand, hug a tree, or sit in the dirt to soak up some of this natural frequency.

Once you start to absorb this healthy vibration from the elements in nature in your body, you are restored and reminded that you are meant to live in this same nurturing flow despite what is normalized back home.

Whatever you can do to connect with your external environment and begin to grow roots from your internal wellspring will be deeply beneficial in this second phase of retreat. Grounding is what quells the anxious excitement so you can start to allow for a greater depth of sustainable energy. It is grounding work that sets the stage for your mental and emotional wellness in the next phase of retreat.

Chapter 19

PHASE 3:
OLD HABITS

Affirmation: I embrace pleasure, passion, and abundance. I celebrate my creative potential and welcome supportive connections into my life.

"So what is the objective of this retreat? What outcomes should I focus on prior to our departure?" Becca asked me before leaving for our retreat.

Hmmm, I thought to myself. How can I convey the fact that you have to let go of the outcomes in order for deeper wisdom to bubble forth while on retreat?

So I told her just that. And thankfully, Becca took a risk, trusted me, and opened herself up for a different kind of experience. A forty-two-year-old single mom of two elementary school–aged kids and a pediatric physical therapist and researcher, Becca rarely had time for herself to do anything that didn't have clear and measurable outcomes.

Becca decided to join the retreat because she wanted to gain some perspective for herself on how to manifest a healthy, long-term relationship after recovering from her divorce. She loved the idea of going somewhere fun and new.

My weeklong retreats always include a day of silence. Becca spent that day completely content within herself—journaling from her bungalow, writing by the juice bar with a smoothie in hand, and walking on the beach. Though a social woman by nature, Becca was surprised by how easy it was to be silent and just with herself.

But then a drastic change surfaced.

As the sun began to set, Becca recounts,

> I remember feeling like a curtain was dropping down over
> me. I felt super crabby and didn't want to do anything—
> dinner with the group, evening activities, none of it. I also
> remember being really sad, and I wasn't sure why after I'd
> had such a great day.
>
> I told Brie I didn't have interest in the evening activi-
> ties because I didn't want to and because I didn't want to
> bring my negative energy to the group. She graciously gave
> me her support in whatever I chose but encouraged me to
> reconsider joining the group for the "breaking the silence"
> ceremony.

Becca then went back to her room and started tidying her
space, emailing, and scheduling her kids' summer activities. And
then she paused. She said, "I was feeling better in this busy, the
bustle of what had become my habitual 'doing' lifestyle. And
then it occurred to me. Crap. I needed to stop and face what was
coming up. I couldn't busy myself away from myself. Not on this
retreat."

So Becca showed up for the ceremony. She participated in the
activities and allowed herself to cry heavily and hard. A release of
years of pain came rushing forth. Becca let the years of overdoing,
scheduling, and going, going, going at once come to a halt. She
said, "I couldn't 'do' the retreat experience away, nor did I want
to. I sat in the dark *shala* after the ceremony ended and felt lighter
and freer. I repeated to myself, 'I am enough.' And though it was
hard to believe, I know now this is exactly why I was on retreat.
This was my moment of insight and growth. And I came pretty
dang close to missing it."

O O O

Phase 3 of retreat is *old habits and anxiousness*. This phase brings
with it a clashing of consciousness. I refer to this stage of retreat
as "hitting the wall." Your old patterns and ways of being from

home crash into the new person you want to be here, on retreat, at this very moment.

Just like Becca, we often try to "do" the retreat in a manner we've been operating back home. You realize quickly that you can't. Despite your overwhelming enthusiasm just days or even moments before, in this phase, you come crashing down.

It is inevitable that you will "hit the wall" at some point on your retreat. And walls take on all sorts of impressive disguises to knock you off course during your retreat experience.

Your wall may show up as the following: *This place is so uncomfortable. I am always freezing at night. I am so bored; what's the point of this anyway? I hate the guide of this program. I don't need this work. I'm already spiritual enough as it is. I miss my kids. I hate the heat.* And on, and on, and painfully on.

These are all covers for *get me the hell out of here. I am struggling to be with myself right now.* Thankfully, Becca recognized this and didn't miss out. And understanding that this stage is a natural experience while retreating will help you recognize your own walls.

Walls are precursors to your breakthroughs. But it is far easier to project your challenges onto external circumstances than it is to witness how you are behaving as a result of them. So this is how we squirm. And this is why we hit the wall on retreat.

A wall can last a brief moment or a few days or it can come up multiple times throughout the course of your retreat. What's important to remember is that your walls are metaphorical. They are not real. They are reflections of your internal landscape, nothing more.

The sooner you can recognize them as such, the sooner you can move through them to your beautiful, new, butterfly self. We all have them, no matter how much work we've done on ourselves. Retreating, in a very safe and intentional environment, triggers walls for the purpose of growth.

The reason walls arise is because of that sneaky ego, or *little me* self. It wants to get caught up in the details and drama and keep you fixed as who you were before you started your retreat and resist change.

You can't blame the ego. After all, that's its job: to create solidity in who we are, what we're about, what we like and don't like, and so on. We can't escape our ego because it serves a biological, protective function. It's there to help us process our external world and find security in who we are. It uses frequent judgment to help us do so.

Problems arise if you get too comfy with your notion of "self" and the very concept of change triggers something deep within you. As a result, you live your life in need of constant certainty and control, which makes for a lot of undue suffering. You cannot control everything around you, though *little me* craves it so.

Retreats are meant to shift, stir, and awaken change in you.

So at this point on retreat, *little me* acts up *big time*. You feel pushed in one way or another because this environment, these people, this amount of stillness, or this pace is so different from what you're used to. And *little me* wants that comfort of certainty.

You must be careful to not place too much significance in your walls. Focusing on your wall that comes up is an easy escape button. It's a way to pull the focus away from what your own areas of growth are and put it onto something external.

Work to stay open and as fluid as you can while on your retreat. During this phase, just as Becca did, recognize your wall instead as a mirror to answer the question, *What part of me is resisting this? Why am I resisting this now?*

You are not on retreat to get taken down by your walls. You are on retreat to take them down. The wall that comes up is your little nugget of truth. It is the exact moment you need to get to your own next level. Encrypted in the challenge is a diamond of clarity. Your own essential lesson sits on the inside, shrouded in the disguise of pain or discomfort.

Your *little me* self says, *Run, run, run! Project, project, project! Obsess, obsess, obsess!* Or whatever form you use most frequently back home. But your *Big me* self says one word once and says it with certainty: *stay.*

Whatever you do, stay. Don't pull out or shut down. This pain is the way to your lesson. Dig in.

Furthermore, it's often the particular projecting coping mechanism that we use at home that appears while on retreat. So this can be massively insightful if we stay with the discomfort. Uncovering "what you do when you're pushed" while on retreat can have huge implications for how to manage your life more skillfully at home.

When we learn to stay with ourselves, amid the feelings of resistance on retreat, our greatest breakthroughs unfold before our very eyes. So long as you feel safe, even if you're not too keen on your bed or guide or the climate, there are incredibly powerful lessons waiting to be unlocked during this very phase.

CHAKRA

In phase 3 of retreat, consider the spiritual connection to your second chakra, your sacral chakra: *Svadhishthana* in Sanskrit. The second chakra resonates with how you relate to others as well as your sense of personal choice. It relates to pleasure and what you enjoy in the world, as well as sexual pleasure. The color associated with the second chakra is orange, like the birth of a new sunrise bringing forth a new day in your life.

The physical location of this energetic center is the lower abdomen, below the navel. So it literally and symbolically represents the seat of your creative center, where you birth new ideas. You have the power to create the life you want, so long as you manage your *little me* self and continue to allow creativity to flow through you.

Problems come in this area of the body or psyche when you feel stifled creatively or powerless in relationships or endeavors in the outside world. Focusing only on the needs of *little me*, though initially may make you feel like you have control, will render you powerless.

You cannot control everything in your external world, and your retreat will remind you of this. Watching your reaction to discomfort from the seat of the witness during this phase of retreat will help keep you balanced and engaged in the process of your unfolding.

A second chakra question that comes up in this phase of retreat is, *How do I respond when I feel like I don't have total control?*

ENERGY

During this stage of retreat, there is a natural dip in energy. You are coming off anxious excitement from the phase prior to this one—an energy level that is not sustainable for the long term. You haven't accessed your deep sense of energy as a result of the entire retreat yet, and the natural response to extremely elevated energy is depleted energy.

This coincides with the sense of discomfort you feel internally, as you're trying to sort out a new way of being yet still hanging on to who you were before you joined this retreat.

Feeling challenged by an external trigger brings your energy down and makes you question everything—your surroundings, yourself, and your decision to come in the first place.

Rest easy knowing this dip in energy is only temporary. It is also very normal and expected. If you do the work of staying with yourself, this small blip will be the very catalyst to catapult you into your infinite pool of energy reserves.

ANTIDOTE

Because you are working with your *old habits* and ways of being in this phase and they're bumping up with who you want to be going forward, the antidote for this phase of retreat is *acknowledgment*.

This phase is one of the reasons it's important to discuss the inner trajectory of retreat. If you know going into your retreat that you're going to experience a lull in energy and emotion at some point, and you know this is the very sign that your insight is coming, you can start to use and view this challenge as a gift.

When you acknowledge that you feel like crap, or you're not as excited as you once were, or things aren't going as planned, you allow your own voice to be heard. You don't play into these stories, of course, but you do your best to recognize them, acknowledge them, and remind yourself that they are only fleeting thoughts. They can move through you.

On longer retreats with my participants, I like to use this phase to look more specifically at our habits and central relationships back home. We start by examining our relationship with our parents. Were they involved, not involved? How does your relationship with your most significant caregivers influence you even now? How have you created who you are today as a result of these primary relationships? And can you leave behind some of what you don't want related to these relationships?

Because the second chakra theme has to do with relating to others and your sense of choice, exploring your relationship with your parents and acknowledging and releasing patterns you've been holding on to unconsciously during this time is greatly beneficial for retreatants. This makes way for participants to be more discerning in what they'd like to carry forward as opposed to just enacting certain behaviors because of history.

No matter how deep you go in this phase and whether you're with an organized program or on your own, give yourself some grace in this period. Acknowledge how you feel and go easy on yourself. Don't allow yourself to be pulled out of your trajectory by overobsessing about the wall that's presenting itself. But allow yourself to move slowly, feel yucky, question your rationale, or feel uneasy in the group.

You are reshaping yourself, and this "breakdown" is an essential step in order to soften your firm sense of who you are so you can be more malleable and intentional when the time comes to rebuild the life you want.

So rest easy. Your resistance is a sign that incredible insights are coming your way. As long as you stay and let the discomfort arise during this phase, you can trust that your struggle is a sign that extraordinary breakthroughs are just around the corner.

Chapter 20

PHASE 4: AWARENESS

Affirmation: I am confident in all that I do. I honor the power within me. I am at peace with myself and the universe.

Lynne was a regular retreat attendant. She came to her first retreat with me seeking new meaning for the next phase in her life. She had a successful career running her own business. After thirty years, she sold her company and found herself asking, *What is next in life?*

She feared she'd sold her identity and relevance along with her business. Lynne wanted to feel good about this next stage of life and sort out these painful feelings. So she sought my retreats to reidentify who she wanted to be next as she transitioned into retirement and turned seventy.

As a regular participant, Lynne knew what to expect throughout the course of the weeklong retreat. She looked forward to the *day of silence* because she knew that it was during this day that she had time to reconnect with her inner voice, journal, read, and think.

For much of her life, she stayed busy. She'd raised three kids, run her business, and never felt entitled to allow herself time to slow down and pause. Though it wasn't until later in life that she started retreating, she was thrilled to have this new practice and committed to doing it at least once per year.

The first time Lynne joined my retreat, she opted to go shopping instead of holding silence. The friend that joined her wanted to shop, and though Lynne felt pulled to stay at the retreat center and hold silence, she didn't want to hurt her friend's feelings.

Instantly, she regretted it. Once she arrived in town, she explained to her friend that she wanted to try the silence and walked back to the center alone. Since that time, Lynne looks forward to the day of silence each year.

It was only after missing the silence on her first experience of retreat that Lynne uncovered how meaningful the practice was for her. Each subsequent retreat, she's held firm to the practice of silence and has fine-tuned how to best experience and frame her day. As an identified extrovert, practicing silence isn't always easy for Lynne. But she believes deeply in the value of it, so she stays with it.

Lynne spends the day doing yoga, journaling, and going out into nature, and when she starts to yearn for more connection, she plays soothing music for herself. She loves looking through old journals and past manuals from retreats to see just how far she's come. Every time she uncovers something new about herself.

Lynne says of the practice of silence,

I continue to be surprised by what I learn about myself when I have nothing to do but be with myself and journal. It is a gift to sit quietly and listen to my inner voice. I find out how I've changed, what I truly want, and what I truly need.

I would encourage every woman to take time to retreat and to hold silence. How else do you pull your head up and figure out if you are who you want to be and if you are living your life with intention?

○ ○ ○

Phase 4 of retreat is *awareness*. It is a very tender step in your process of self-awakening and arguably the most important. You just hit a low in phase 3 of retreat. Whether you noticed the dip in your energy, your enthusiasm, or your attitude, something pushed you to the edge of yourself. In the last section, we spoke about "staying with yourself" when you felt that rub. But how exactly do you stay with yourself during your pain? What does this mean in practice?

Phase 4 of retreat is so important because it's where you build your emotional muscle and strengthen your spirit to make way for your beautiful future. In the previous phase, your *little me* self did everything possible to try to pull you out of focus and place blame on everything external. *Little me* threw a big fit.

And now, like the calm of a toddler in his mother's arms after a massive meltdown, you hold yourself tightly. Let the wave of resistant emotion move through you. You witness everything around and in you with profound clarity. You stay in this pause and witness, without judgment, as much as you can.

Hopefully, your resistance gave you an opportunity to move and clear old, unwanted energy. That's all resistance ever is: a surge of energy. You can attach yourself to this energy, keep it stuffed down inside of you, build an identity around it, create your reality as a result of it. Or you can let it move through you, as energy is meant to do.

You'll know you've entered phase 4 when you're willing to let that rush of energy move through you and watch as your inner ocean calms, like the waves after a rainstorm. You'll notice you've arrived when you stop fighting so strongly. When you drop the battle and surrender to what is unfolding rather than what you are forcing. When you start to allow and settle into this new energy and it doesn't feel so hard anymore, you are in phase 4.

Here you can see with profound clarity. So you intentionally bask in this phase before you welcome the energy of others. You may feel too fragile at this point to share your vulnerable luminosity, so make the space to be quiet and only with yourself in phase 4 of retreat.

CHAKRA

The third chakra, the solar plexus chakra—*Manipura* in Sanskrit—is what we thematically relate to in phase 4 of retreat. It represents the seat of your personal power, governing self-awareness, and self-esteem. This chakra represents how you relate to yourself and how you digest things physically, mentally, and emotionally.

Located between the belly button and the breastbone, this chakra is associated with the color yellow or gold. The theme of this chakra is learning to relate with yourself. It relates so perfectly to our trajectory because this is the time when you stay with yourself with a deep sense of awareness.

You have the opportunity here to know yourself better, to relate with yourself in a healthier fashion. One that is more intentional and truer as opposed to mirroring your environment back home. You can take back control at this point in retreat. And you choose how and what you'll digest to allow for your transformation to unfold. Third chakra questions that arise in this phase of retreat are, *What do I want? How do I envision my life separate from everyone in it?*

ENERGY

Energy in phase 4 of retreat begins to steadily build. It is certainly higher than it was when you were internally fighting yourself in the previous stage. But because you are in new and foreign territory with yourself, you have not yet rebounded to where you were in phase 2.

Furthermore, it is critically important in this phase to manage your energy and stay by yourself. At least for a bit. It is a vulnerable time, and you are dealing with fertile ground within yourself. Welcoming energy from others, media of any kind, or anything that poses a threat to influence you in this stage should be avoided. Keep guard at the door of your mind, emotions, and energy in this phase of retreat.

You must be protective of your energy here. In this stage, you begin to use your energy as your own medicine and notice what that feels like. Instead of splaying your energy onto everyone and everything around you, you hold on to it for your own personal inquiry.

In this phase, energy begins the authentic ascent to where it will be at the end of your retreat. But you must create the foundation in this stage in order for the rise of energy to be continuous and complete and built on solid ground.

In this phase, your eyes are wide open and you direct your focus on yourself. You nurture yourself, ask guided questions of yourself, and answer in your mind and journal. You allow the deep dive to be completely about yourself.

This can feel indulgent, especially for women, who make so much of our focus about everything outside of us. Yet it is essential. It is how you begin to fill your cup. You must know and fill yourself before you can know and fill anyone else.

But you must find your inner resolve if growth is what you seek. Sit still. Let it burn. Be bored. Be alone. Get to know and hear yourself again. The pause is worth the pain in the long run.

It takes discipline and grit to force a pause when your surroundings tell you to do everything but. But you know better than to be a victim to your environment. You are the creator of your life. The liver of your dreams. So you choose to withhold for the sake of your one precious life.

ANTIDOTE

In order to propel your sense of awareness and ultimate transformation as a result of your retreat, you use *silence* as the antidote in this phase. Just as protecting your energy is critical here in order to really know yourself, silence is critical in order to fully hear yourself.

When you begin to feel yourself calm down after the last stage of resistance, find a way to hold the silence for yourself. This is one of the most productive ways to hear yourself.

On your own, this is easy. In a group setting, this can be difficult. But it is essential. Many experiences that claim to be retreats tend toward parties or tours more than actual retreats, where participants spend every down moment socializing.

There is nothing wrong with socializing—it can be delightful and fun. But so much more is possible if personal growth is what you seek. This doesn't mean you have to write off a retreat experience as a failure if you realize you are on a "party-style" retreat. It just means you have to work harder to find places to hold silence and stillness for yourself. This can be in silent mornings or sunset beach walks, solo hikes in the mountains, meals taken alone, and more. Use your creativity. Be sure to ask your retreat guide prior to your experience what kind of space there is for silence.

Of course, many people resist silence. In a culture that prizes instant gratification, it seems dull and boring. Why be quiet when I can be connecting with others? Again, if growth is what you're after, some element of withholding is critical. Very rarely in life do we withhold. Especially in Western culture. Silence is an easy opportunity that gives you direct pathways to your own sense of self if you have the discipline to try it.

But silence on its own won't provide growth. For example, if you fritter away your silent time on the internet, you'll miss out on a critical opportunity to listen to yourself. If you jump from one distraction to another, you run the risk of evading the self completely. Be careful of easy indulgences that are normalized back home while on retreat. You are here not to repeat unhealthy patterns but to build new and nourishing ones.

This is why *silence* is the antidote for *awareness* in phase 4 of retreat. It is certainly nice to come home with wonderful social connections and having had a great time. But in the end, you want to feel energetically alive and powerful by the end of your retreat so you can go home even more empowered. Socializing in every spare moment keeps the energy on the external, while a retreat with some element of silence gives you the chance to build the internal flame.

This phase will not be easy for everyone. As I mentioned, often initially there is resistance. And for some, even during the allotted time of silence there will be push back. Some people hit their walls amid silence.

But the momentary act of withholding allows your energy and insights to build to an explosive level, one that, after the fact, is worth every moment of struggle, as you'll learn in phase 5 of retreat.

Chapter 21

PHASE 5: NEW FREQUENCY

Affirmation: I am love. I radiate this essence. I allow love to fill and guide me.

Sixty-three-year-old Jada signed up for retreat with trepidation in her heart. She had not taken many retreats in her life and wasn't sure how much of herself she wanted to reveal.

Yet she knew she was at a critical point in her life and needed something to remind her of her inner wisdom, beauty, and power. Her new marriage was struggling, and her body was in pain from a recent back injury. She had just sold the house she built, designed, and adored to create a fresh life with her new husband.

Jada had a thriving career creating and designing beautiful homes for others. Though she was experiencing countless professional wins, something inside her felt lost and out of touch with herself.

Jada celebrated the chance for a *day of silence.* A spiritually inclined woman and artist, she was delighted by the opportunity to embrace her aloneness. She soaked up every moment of the day, sitting alone at meals to fully experience the potential of the silent spaciousness.

Once it was finally time to reunite as a group after the *day of silence,* Jada was delighted. The group had grown quite close, so they couldn't wait to speak to each other again and share their experiences. The day after silence, retreatants created a painting in the day and participated in a sacred dance ceremony after the sun set amid a room of lit candles and music to unleash the soul.

Jada says of her experience,

Reuniting with the group after silence was so joyful. I felt buoyant, grounded, and clean. I was ready to share and listen, but even more important, I enjoyed feeling the marination of spirit inside of me.

Seeing other women in their process was fascinating. I wanted to hold each one as though they were my children. I felt that I regained my authentic, solid wisdom. Rather than self-questioning as a deterrent to my power, it became an understanding of how important my life experiences have been for me, empowering me once again. My life is about creativity and light.

Something in Jada cracked open this day. As a result of her retreat, Jada was able to forgive a handful of painful relationships from her past. She says, "I found a true release from the inner chains that bound me to them in a negative way, understanding their inherent goodness and flaws and deeply forgiving them. I now feel more freedom than I've ever felt."

O O O

Phase 5 of retreat is *new frequency*. As a retreat guide, this is absolutely one of my favorite stages to witness in the participants' journey. Because you withheld in the previous phase, you are now literally bursting with energy.

In this phase, participants start to feel the beginnings of what it means to be authentically full. You've just spent a day focusing on yourself with no distractions. You've slowed the pace of your life. You've limited your inputs.

Now your output potential is insurmountable. So long as you participated intentionally in the previous phase of retreat, you will feel a natural emotional lift in this stage. Because you didn't run or distract yourself in your quiet, you now have reserves you didn't even know were possible. A participant can't help but feel delighted by this sense of personal power in phase 5 of retreat.

CHAKRA

The resonant chakra in phase 5 of retreat is chakra 4, your heart chakra: *Anahata* in Sanskrit. It is located in the center of the chest and is associated with the color green. The heart chakra is the bridge between the lower and the upper chakras, blending the physical and the spiritual. So it makes sense that in this phase, your energy would start to lift and lighten as you move from form to spirit, matter to energy, particle to wave.

The fourth chakra represents love, compassion, joy, and inexpressible truths that cannot be recounted in words. And this is when you find yourself beginning to open wide to a new you.

For the first time on retreat, you notice heart and mind coherence. You feel fully aligned with what you feel and what you think, so much so that you begin to witness synchronicities all around you. Before, the glass was murky, and you couldn't see through to the other side. Now you will start to see with clarity because the alignment you feel is real and is intentional as a result of heeding the phases of retreat.

ENERGY

There is a massive surge in energy in this phase of retreat. Whether you're alone or on an organized retreat, if you've followed the previous stages of retreat, you will notice an elevation in physical energy, positive emotion, and spiritual insight during this phase.

If you're part of a group, the collective energy is off the charts. People can't wait to see each other again, the shared conversation is louder and more excitable, and you feel like you could run a marathon, start a business, heal the world, and become the president.

It's really quite something. If you're alone, your inspiration starts to build, new ideas come pouring in, and your outlook and perspective are optimistic and expansive.

And unlike in phase 2, when the energy was synthetic and unsustainable, this time it's authentic. It's real. It comes not from discomfort but from extreme comfort. You feel renewed, full, and completely bathed in love and understanding for both yourself and the deeper truths of your life.

Antidote

The antidote for phase 5 of retreat, *new frequency*, is *creativity and play*. Because your energy and outlook are so drastically heightened in this phase and you are so wildly aligned between your head and heart, you will feel the urge to celebrate your extraordinary expression of life.

It's possible that you may not have felt this alive and aligned since you were a child, when you were still unaware of life's burdens and expectations. In honor of living from your heart, use this stage to be creative and playful, just like a child.

If you haven't felt this vibrant in a while, you may feel a tendency to either spread this energy to everyone/everything around you or try to lock down on it and claim it as "the new you." This is sneaky *little me* at play here trying to either resist (spread your energy everywhere else but you) or attach (claim this as the new you). And it is very tempting because you feel so great.

Instead, I suggest you "dance" with this energy as opposed to resisting or attaching. You use it and let it swirl in and around you, as energy is meant to do. You welcome it, celebrate it, and invite it to continue to flow through your open mind, heart, and physical form.

Your goal here is to remain open. In this phase, you are reminded that the more open you stay, the more access you have to this energy that feels so good right now. So phase 5 shows you your own potential for openness.

For my weeklong women's retreats, each phase is celebrated on a particular day. The day for phase 5 is notoriously known by my participants as "vagina day." It is all about reconnecting with pleasure, as our vaginas so beautifully symbolize. Participants often feel silly and giggle as I introduce the day. But this keeps them out of their analytical minds. It keeps them open, fluid, and playful.

We make art, have a ritual dance ceremony, and let go of "the work" for a day. We remember the playful nature of our inner child; we bring her out and light the retreat site ablaze with our laughter and pleasure. Through these lessons, we remember how far we have strayed from desire and pleasure to *should* and *must* and *have to* in our daily lives back home. We train ourselves to go back to the old ways.

We remember that our birthright as women is to experience pleasure. As Regena Thomashauer reminds us, there are 8,000 nerve endings in the clitoris.[1] There's not another part of the body, male or female, that has even 150. If that doesn't convince us that women are meant to experience pleasure, I don't know what does.

The lessons that come out of this day for participants are profound. A woman realizes she's lost the play in her marriage, and it's running dry as a result. An executive realizes what she really wants was to become an artist, too, and visual depictions come rushing into her mind the moment she remembers. A mom uncovers that she's been commanding her kids to be militantly disciplined as opposed to letting them squeal and wrestle and run naked, as they desire. And they each decide to change their ways the moment they walk in the door at home after the retreat.

These are the little shifts you uncover from playing and creating and enjoying that have massive impacts on your life. By honoring your own light heart, you can lighten and uplift the entire world around you.

It is through creating, playing, and enjoying pleasure that you find your way back to yourself in this phase. When you embrace the femininity within you, whether male, female, or nonbinary, you remember that life can be joyous, delightful, hilarious, beautiful, and fluid. And not only do you think this is so; you embody it down to your very nature as a result of phase 5 of retreat.

Chapter 22

PHASE 6: EPIPHANY

Affirmation: I speak up for myself. I express myself with clarity and confidence. I step toward what is true, and I express my gratitude for life.

Ella originally came to my IGNITE Retreat on a work assignment. Her company was considering offering retreats for their employees, and Ella was tasked to research and experience a retreat of her own. She would then come back and report how relevant she thought it could be for her company.

Ella spent many years in the fitness industry and had a life she was proud of. At fifty-seven years young, she had two grown children and a healthy relationship she valued with her second husband. Ella came to the retreat ready to take a break for herself and soak up as much information as she could for her team.

After settling into the routine of morning silence, yoga, the Heart Curriculum workshop, and regular dips into the natural hot springs, she felt herself fully relaxing. Yet as much as this was a work trip for Ella, it quickly started to feel personal too.

During her free time one day, Ella walked out to the on-site labyrinth carrying a heavy question that had been with her for years. One she hadn't planned on addressing here, now.

Can I forgive my ex-husband?

Ella had been married before, for twenty-three years. Her first husband was the father of her two children, and the marriage ended nearly thirteen years before. Her divorce was painful and public as a result of her husband's illegitimate business dealings. This elicited feelings of shame, humiliation, and self-doubt for Ella. She was a strong and successful woman and mother, so she kept these feelings inside in order to protect herself and others.

These hidden feelings prevented her from having a genuine relationship with anyone, including her second husband. Her private pain left her feeling tired, lonely, and overwhelmed. But at the opening ceremony on the first night, Ella knew this retreat would be her opportunity to peel back what had been haunting her for years if only she was open enough to do so.

As Ella began walking the labyrinth that day after a morning silence, she let the feeling of her feet touching the earth resonate in her body. Answers for thirteen years of pain started to come to her as if out of nowhere.

She was not responsible for her ex-husband's behavior or decisions. People had tried to express their concern for her for years during their marriage, but she hadn't been ready to hear it. And despite how excruciating her burden was, she was not meant to continue to carry this burden forever.

The phrase that came to Ella over and over again was "You have to forgive in order to live." Ella recounts,

> When I reached the center of the labyrinth I was crying big, deep, soul-cleansing sobs. I let go of the girl who had been swept off her feet by a charismatic young man who made her feel so special. I let go of the woman who tried to make everything right when his actions were inappropriate, wrong, and spirit wounding. I released the woman who kept going no matter what because if she stopped, then that would mean she was a failure at being a wife and mother. I lay down and cradled the Ella who just wanted to love her husband and be loved back and have the family she worked so hard to pull together.

After some time alone, Ella stood up with the question, "Are you ready?" Ella remembers,

I looked to the sky, seeing the openness of the space above me. I looked toward the beautiful Colorado mountains, seeing the power and strength next to me. I felt compelled to begin walking toward my life as I released all of the hurt and anger and pain into the center of the labyrinth.

The walk to the opening of the labyrinth was quick. But because I was being moved forward, having released a massive emotional load, a lightness allowed me to float to the entrance. I knew as soon as I exited the labyrinth, I would be me again, not just a half-open shell with a strong protective cover.

Without looking back, my new journey had begun.

o o o

Hopefully, in some way or another, you honored your inner playful child in the previous phase of retreat. Perhaps you danced, played, or made some art. Now it is time to get about the business of making your retreat have lasting impact on your life.

Retreats are meant to be at first healing, then playful and fun, and finally, transformative. And so this next phase is so incredibly critical on your retreat. Phase 6 of retreat is *epiphany*.

Because you were so wildly open to the energy naturally flowing through you in the previous phase of retreat, you are vibing on a whole new level. You are now ready to sculpt this energy to serve you in your life back home.

In this phase, you are stepping ever closer to your reentry to "normal" life. You begin to think about seeing your family, going back to work, integrating what you've learned about yourself on your retreat into your life back home.

It would be a waste of momentum, energy, and luminosity to not use your retreat experience to breathe new life into your world back home and to take some kind of action. So it is during this phase of retreat that you start to ask yourself some important questions and make some plans about who you will reenter the world as upon your return.

By now, you've likely had multiple breakthroughs and insights about yourself and your personal life. It is common in this stage of retreat to have numerous radical insights as you start to think about your life back home.

These profound insights inspire subtle shifts and actions that will have a significant impact on your life. Some of the breakthroughs will be logistical: you might realize how much happier you are with a meditation practice each morning and commit to doing it at home too. You might learn that having a fresh smoothie for breakfast makes you far more productive than your typical bowl of cereal. The habits you've benefited from on retreat are ones you'd like to bring into your life once you return.

And some of your breakthroughs will be spiritual. Like Ella, you may finally be ready to forgive for something that's gutted you for decades. You might realize you can no longer stay with a partner that doesn't appreciate you. You might decide to pursue your dream of being a designer despite the stable paycheck you receive from your corporate job. Or you might commit to going back to school even though everyone has told you you're too old.

This phase is when you give your retreat meaning. An experience that transforms your consciousness is beautiful, but you'll only transform your life if you take action in your day-to-day back home.

In Phase 6 of Retreat, you'll answer the questions, *So what does all of this mean? What am I actually going to do about all my insights and breakthroughs?*

CHAKRA

Phase 6 of retreat aligns with the fifth Chakra, the throat chakra: *Vishuddha* in Sanskrit. The fifth chakra is located at the throat and is connected to the thyroid, parathyroid, jaw, mouth, neck, tongue, and larynx. It is associated with the color blue and is the first of the three spiritual chakras.

The spiritual intent of the fifth chakra is all about expressing your truth, which fits perfectly with this stage.

By now, you have uncovered and released what you have been suppressing. You've changed your vibration, and you're starting to think more about what you want your future to look like.

When you are so focused on pleasing, whether it be your family, your boss, or some internalized societal ideal, you often stray further and further from speaking what you really feel. Healing this chakra has everything to do with expressing what is authentic even if it is not what others want to hear. When you can align your inside thoughts with your outside expressions, you will live your most powerful life.

This takes extreme courage. So you'll need to be intentional about envisioning how you'll manifest your new expressions back home, down to the logistics of what your new routines will be. Be very specific about what changes you want to make once you reenter your life. The more specific, the more likely it is to happen as a result of your clarity. At this stage, it is time to speak and claim your truth.

ENERGY

For the last two phases, you've been on a steady incline, energetically. What begins to happen at stage 6 is you not only feel your energy increase, vertically; you feel it expand, horizontally. Something at home that once drained you completely now gives you a feeling of renewed energy when thinking about it. You have a multitude of new ideas to put in place once you get home.

This does not come as a result of thinking about your challenges long and hard for a number of days on your retreat. It comes from the natural insight that giving yourself space allows. Because you held firm boundaries and have continuously taken care of yourself first, you now have a burst of ideas to handle any challenge.

From an inner energetic perspective, if you've followed the suggestion of frequent daily meditations up to now, you have trained yourself to readily access the alpha brainwave state. When you know how to go here easily, your brain becomes more universal, with big ideas, than in your regularly lived survival state, known as beta brainwave state. From the slower, more consistent, relaxed, alpha brain wave state, you can solve any challenge. *This* is *Big me* thinking.

So at this phase, what were once your problems back home become your fuel. Solutions come like a showering of shooting stars, and this gives you incredible amounts of energy. What once held you back now serves as your very propellant to thrust you forward.

With energy like this, you can solve or handle anything. And this is why this stage is called *epiphany*.

ANTIDOTE

The antidote for stage 6 of retreat is *transmute and manifest*. Now the real work, the work that has the potential to shift your life completely, takes place. During this stage, you take action so your retreat is more than just a nice experience.

On retreats I host, participants decide during this phase what their extraordinary futures will be. Not just mentally but somatically. I use everything from goal setting to visualizing, vocalizing, embodied movements, archetype work, mission statements, creating new personal or family values, and action plans. Whatever strategy works to bring about the most action is what you should use for yourself here.

If living your best life is what you seek, you have to be reborn over and over again. Going home, there is real risk in just settling back into what is easy and comfortable. But then you are not living to your full potential. Your retreat was meant to break your patterns, shake up your normal just a tad.

Manifesting is not just a mental game. It's a practice of discipline and action. If you've benefited from being away on your retreat, you owe it to yourself and to the people who made it possible for you to leave to make tangible and specific changes once you enter life back home.

Of course, you can't always predict how life is going to go once you get home. But you can control yourself. So whatever action you can take on your own, independent of your loved ones or your environment, you commit to it now, in phase 6 of retreat.

This is what makes a retreat different from a travel experience or a social, party-style retreat. Ask yourself the question, *So what am I going to do?* Ask it multiple times, and write the answers in your journal. What is going to change when I get home? How will I be different once I get home?

Take the time to do this work. Whether you're in a group or alone, find the space to think through your answers. This is how you manifest your new reality. This is how you transmute what once was pain into power and manifest incredible feats at home. Do the work here and have your retreat serve you for months, even years to come.

Chapter 23

PHASE 7:
GRATITUDE

Affirmation: I am connected to the divine source of the universe. I honor and follow my intuition and invite sacred transformation.

Erica was delighted to have some time for herself on retreat. A single, thirty-nine-year-old business executive, she had a pace of life that had been excruciatingly fast for the past ten years. Though she was nervous that her respite would leave her woefully behind with her duties and obligations at work, her fears quickly melted away when she arrived at the retreat center and began her retreat experience.

Erica came to the retreat with a completely open mind. She'd had breakthroughs and insights all week long about how to better care for herself, her family, her friends, and her team at work. She created a new morning routine that included meditation and journaling at the start of each day, one that she kept the entire retreat and in the subsequent months back home. Erica had found her way back to herself.

On the final day of retreat, Erica had a chance to reflect on the work we did related to her family. When the time came to write a letter of gratitude to someone in her life, without hesitation, she chose her father.

Growing up, Erica had always identified more closely with her mother. This retreat had given her a chance to reflect on all the positive ways her father impacted her life too. He was an avid outdoorsman and athlete, and she had gained this trait from him too. He was intelligent, well-read, funny, and solitary. He was a leader in his industry, just like she was. Being away on retreat made Erica realize all the many ways she appreciated her father.

All of these things and more Erica included in her letter to her father. It was a teary experience for Erica but one that she felt brought her even closer to him. She couldn't wait to share it with him and see his response.

When she returned home, she shared what she wrote in her letter with her dad. She expressed with him sentiments she had never shared before. It felt good to vocalize and honor big feelings of love and gratitude for him in this way, Erica remembers.

Her dad, a man of few words, humbly listened and took in what his daughter had never before expressed to him.

Unexpectedly and suddenly, just six months after Erica returned from her retreat, her father passed away. Devastated, Erica's entire family grieved at how quickly they lost their patriarch.

Erica still feels the dull ache of her father's absence. She says of how taking the time for this gratitude on retreat impacted her:

It's so hard to put into words. I just feel so profoundly grateful that I communicated my love and gratitude from that letter to my father while he was still alive.

I feel like I don't have to carry regret because I thought about and said how much he meant to me. If it weren't for the retreat, I don't know if I would have thought about him so intentionally in this way. I'm just so deeply thankful.

O O O

You have reached the near-final stages of your retreat. Perhaps it's the last day or few days. You look back on your time, and you can't believe how quickly it's gone by. You remember the trepidation you had to come on retreat, and you know that was a different you.

You are changed. Renewed. Healed. Inspired. Down to your very core, you feel full and actually ready to go home and jump back into your life.

Gratitude is the seventh phase of retreat. Here, you allow your-self to reflect on your experience. You look back on your time and recount the ups and the downs. You look at them with pleasure knowing they were all a part of your journey to bring you to who you are and how you feel in this very moment.

You can't help but be overwhelmed with gratitude for the life that led you to this moment. For the people who supported you, for the new you that is still evolving. You finally feel connected to who you were meant to be again. Without distractions, you've found your way back to yourself.

And like Erica, you may feel compelled to share your love with the important people in your life. As her story reminds us, we never know when we'll no longer be able to do so. So this work is not only healthy; it's literally life changing.

When you feel gratitude, you cannot simultaneously feel feel-ings of anger, resentment, fear, insecurity, or any of the other dis-empowering emotions people often find themselves overcome by.

This stage is important to frame your entire experience. When you continue to practice feeling gratitude, you will continue to see more to be grateful for. This is a beautiful new pattern to go home with. And that is why this stage is essential on your retreat-ing journey.

CHAKRA

The sixth chakra—*Ajna* in Sanskrit—is often referred to as the third-eye center. *Ajna* means "command," and this chakra is situated in between and just above the eyes. It's associated with the pineal gland and is often referred to as the seat of the soul, or the seat of intuition.

The spiritual intention of this chakra has to do with learning to see a higher perspective. This syncs perfectly with stage 7 of retreat because you've finally healed your-self. Now you can see beyond just yourself to understand how this new, more evolved, healthy, and happy version of you can transition back into life at home.

In this stage and through this chakra, you no longer project your wounded ego, or *little me* self. By now, you're literally starting to lift your head up and see the bigger picture. You no longer exist only in your stressful state; that has had time to unwind and harmonize with your inner vibration of well-being.

You feel strong and not so mired by past pains, limiting beliefs, and disempowering habit patterns. From here, as you access a healed sixth chakra, you begin to see things as they are and are able to move forward with more congruence and efficiency in your life.

ENERGY

Energy continues to climb here because you feel so full of your own clear seeing. You no longer feel stifled by the struggles that ailed you just prior to this retreat. You have boundless energy to use for your own good and the good of those around you. At this stage of retreat, you feel powerful thinking about how you'll share your new way of being in your life back home.

And this power unlocks your unlimited reserves of energy and inspiration. When you live from this state of inspiration and action, you realize your energy aligns and makes itself available for anything at all that you dream of.

Energy wants to serve and move through that which is living and thriving. And you are absolutely thriving in this stage of retreat. So copious amounts of energy continue to be available for you. When you live in alignment with heart and mind, your energy is synchronized.

Instead of battling against conflicting thoughts, feelings, and emotions, they are vibrating in one concurrent flow. As a result, you feel unbelievable amounts of energy and personal power in this stage.

ANTIDOTE

The antidote for phase 7 of retreat is *forgive, purify, and celebrate*. Because your energy and power are so elevated, you can use this opportunity to forgive. It is my experience working with hundreds of people through my retreats, yoga, and coaching that forgiveness is one of the greatest emotional challenges for us humans. But now is exactly the right time to put it into practice.

Because you're feeling better than you've ever felt at this stage, it's important to use your energy and insight for long-term personal growth. Feeling emotionally and spiritually elevated is fantastic. But if you go home still carrying grudges, you have not done the extent of the work that is possible on retreat.

So it is important during this time to forgive, to finally lay down the sword. It may be, after looking at your past, you realize you've been hanging on to resentment for a parent or sibling. Maybe it's a lover or boss that's done you wrong, and you haven't been able to shake it. Or maybe you need to forgive yourself.

Either way, intentionally forgiving creates more spaciousness within yourself. It can only truly be done from elevated levels of consciousness. So you must use the state of grace you're now experiencing to forgive.

The second antidotal step in this phase of retreat is to purify. In a sense, forgiving is purifying. Absolutely. However, I believe that feelings of resentment, anger, and many other disempowering emotions are not always transparent to the mind but carried only in our bodies. Sometimes, we've shoved our pain down so deeply that thinking about it and bringing it into our consciousness isn't even a possibility.

On retreats that I host, for this phase, I always have participants do some form of somatic release to move any last bits of blocked energy that are no longer processed through the mind rather only through the body. I use all kinds of techniques—from yelling, to punching a pillow, to throwing something, anything that aggressively moves strong and buried energy away from the body.

For women, in particular, this is critical. Women are rarely allowed to be fierce, angry, rageful, and vengeful. Societally, we are taught to be proper and polite, obliging, quiet, and pleasant. We tell our little girls to calm down and be sweet.

So we have years of stored rage just waiting to come out. Allowing for some sort of somatic release helps you move stagnant energy that you're storing deep in the recesses of your cells that needs to move in order to free yourself and create even more buoyancy in your consciousness and physical form.

My suggestion with this kind of work is to do it briefly and then come back to gratitude. We don't want to color all the energy and momentum we've worked so hard to build throughout the course of our retreat with pain and anger and rage. Definitely, these are important to feel. But this is not an exercise of the mind; we've done that part already by now. This is an exercise purely of the body.

So release something. Make it strong, aggressive, and powerful. And then come back to gratitude. Try a mantra after doing your release: "My heart is full of love and understanding. My heart is full of love and understanding." Or come up with your own loving incantation that's filled with grace, forgiveness, and gratitude.

Finally, you celebrate in this phase of retreat. As has been discussed throughout this book, whatever you emotionally feel in your body will be mirrored in your external environment.

So allow for feelings of celebration to overtake you. You are a new person as a result of your experience, and this absolutely deserves some celebration! If you are in a group and if you have a great guide, this will likely be taken care of. Perhaps you'll close with a ceremony or ritual. Perhaps you'll share a final meal in delight together.

If you are by yourself, create your own closing ritual. Go back to the spots where you first visited upon your arrival. Walk out to the mountain or go sit on the beach and watch the sun set. Smile and feel gratitude and celebratory feelings in your heart because you are alive and because this is what it feels like to thrive.

Remind yourself that you don't need a reason to feel this good. You've trained yourself to live in this state, and no matter what happens upon your reentry, this very state is accessible at all times. Trust in this truth, and celebrate the new incredible version of yourself you've discovered as a result of your retreat.

Chapter 24

PHASE 8: EMBODY

Affirmation: I am infinite and boundless. I go beyond my limiting beliefs. I am divinely guided and inspired.

Sage was a regular retreat attendant. She'd joined many of my programs before and was delighted to have some time away for herself amid the busyness of raising two kids and running a household.

This time, she came on retreat for a very specific reason: to gain insights about her marriage. Her husband, Danny, had recently left his job and was searching for his next career move. This meant the two of them shared space regularly, much more than either of them was used to.

The two had some marital challenges during their thirteen years together. But when Danny was working, these problems didn't seem quite as pressing. Now, however, with Danny home full-time, Sage and Danny were completely consumed by their issues. Regular arguments broke out, and their children started to develop anxiety as a result of the conflict they witnessed.

Sage was adamant that something had to change. The question was how and what?

Throughout the course of the retreat, Sage dedicated all her efforts to her husband and her marriage. Every meditation, teaching, meal conversation, and moment of alone time, Sage focused her intention on the well-being of her marriage.

A woman who openly and regularly looked at herself, Sage was ready to take ownership of her role in what was making her relationship so difficult. Her free time was spent reading about marriage, journaling, and asking herself what she could do to make the relationship better. And as a result of such focus, breakthroughs and insights abounded.

She realized where she was creating unnecessary problems in the relationship. She decided that having two different parenting styles could work within one family—he could parent his way, and she hers. This didn't need to cause her tension anymore. She uncovered how if she focused on what was great about Danny, instead of what wasn't, they'd be happier as a couple. These were just a few of the insights she gained.

Sage left the retreat inspired to go home and be the very best version of herself for the sake of the relationship. She was ready to share her insights and her newly evolved self with Danny. She couldn't wait to see how the personal shifts she had made and perspectives she'd gained would enliven the relationship.

It didn't take long for Sage to realize that the problems she left with were still there when she returned. She came home thinking she alone would change the relationship. After just a few weeks, she realized that if they were going to make changes, it would require them to both be on board. This was not a one-person job.

Sage conveyed this to Danny, and he agreed to start counseling with her. The Danny she believed she knew was stubborn, arrogant, and unwilling to change. But the Danny that was in front of her postretreat was completely different from her previously held views. Sage says of her retreat experience,

> Turns out, and fortunately for us, I didn't know my husband at all! Without the retreat to set us on this path, I may never have known the truth about my husband or that by working hard on our problems, we could have a new and beautiful version of our marriage.
>
> Had I not been able to step away and look at my marriage and the role that I played with fresh eyes, I would likely still be swimming in that desperate state: at home with kids running around, my husband pushing all of my buttons, life swarming around me in every waking moment.
>
> At home, I was in no position to observe myself in my marriage in a calm and focused manner. I was too "in it"

to see how it could be different. I put so much attention on my marriage during the retreat that there was no way I could go back to the old way at home. This retreat was the opening I needed to allow for this new relationship.

○ ○ ○

This stage of retreat, *embody*, refers to life beyond retreat. This is all about reintegrating home and bringing your newfound energy, insights, clarity, and sense of peace with you back to where you were prior to retreat.

This is when you have the chance to model the new you to the world. It's a vulnerable phase that we'll deep dive into in the final section of this book. How you reintegrate can have massive implications for how long your retreat will serve you after you get home. Unless you're intentional about how you transition back into life, you may quickly find yourself slipping into old patterns that you meant to leave behind.

But filled with this new energy and life from your experience, you have the power to set the stage for life exactly on your terms once you go back home. Just as Sage did with her husband.

CHAKRA

The seventh chakra, the crown chakra—*Sahasrara* in Sanskrit—is located on the top of the head and represents transcendent thinking and our ability to connect with all of life outside ourselves.

When you are aligned with this chakra, you'll feel grateful, fully alive, and filled with inspiration. Of course, this syncs perfectly with the close of your retreat and reintegration with life back home. Your job now is to take all you've learned about yourself and interact with the world to re-create the life you want for yourself postretreat.

ENERGY

During phase 8, you'll feel your highest level of energy yet, but this stage will also require the most energy from you. It is easy to feel elevated and blissful when taking care of yourself is your primary focus throughout the day. When you come back home, you're balancing the energy of other people as well as the other commitments in your life.

You are fully equipped with the energy and insight to manage all of it skillfully. So long as you don't fall back into disempowering habits or relationships, your energy should continue to carry you for many weeks, months, or maybe even a year.

Managing your own energy is a reminder of why retreating is a regular practice of self-care. I recommend *at least* one per year. While retreating keeps energy high for long periods of time, regular tune-ups for yourself are essential.

ANTIDOTE

The antidote for the final phase of retreat is *integrate*. In the next section, we'll look closely at how to do this skillfully to make the benefits of your retreat last long beyond your final day in process.

But as you journey home and think about reuniting with your people and commitments, it's important to think about those who made it possible for you to leave in the first place. You've just had a life-altering experience. You want to share about it, live it, transform the world, which is amazing, and you should do so with gusto.

But often there are people waiting at home whose lives may have been more difficult as a result of you stepping away. Upon returning home, instead of sharing all the profound ways in which you've changed, it's important to ensure your partner and your children or any significant friends or csonnections that you love them and you missed them.

In particular, partners who may have been ambivalent about you leaving might have some unexpressed fear that you may have grown beyond them. Or perhaps they feel it is unfair for you to take time away and not them. Ensure them that you're thankful for all they did to help make your retreat possible. And discuss ideas of how they can leave for their own retreat next. This will create an even stronger sense of connection and equanimity in the partnership moving forward.

Of course, there are many ways to make your reintegration worthwhile and prolong your sense of inspiration and embolden the new you. Let's get into it together in the next section.

PART IV

TRANSITIONING BACK HOME

Chapter 25

WHEN OTHERS NOTICE

I owe everything that I have done to the fact that I am very much at ease being alone.
—Marilynne Robinson, "Marilynne Robinson: The Art of Fiction No. 198"

So you've made it home after your retreat. You've connected with your people. You've exchanged tearful welcome backs, spent time soaking up the love from your children, started to settle in back at work. You feel happy you went and so delighted to be home. Congratulations.

You are glowing. And people around you start to take notice. People you didn't even really know before are suddenly drawn to you. They ask you how your retreat went, and you tell them. As your glow continues, they start to ask you more: "Are you eating anything different? What are you reading? What does your morning routine look like? What shampoo are you using?" and on and on and on.

One of the wildest benefits of retreat is how other people are drawn to you afterward. You've had a complete shift, energetically, as the trajectory in the last section showed. And as we've discussed, when we're open to energy, more of it flows through us, in us, and around us.

Because very few people understand subtle energy (aside from you, now!), yet we all experience it on a visceral level, we cannot help but be pulled to people who have an elevated level of energy. This is exactly what you did on retreat: build your inner energetic reserves.

People in daily life make the mistake of thinking the shift you've made is some kind of external change (*what kind of shampoo are you using, and what are you eating?*). But you know it's all about the inside game. Retreat has the power to shift your inner world. And that's what people are picking up on, believing it may be external.

Knowingly or not, they are drawn to you because they crave this same kind of energy for themselves. It's primitive, really. We all have a deep desire to feel alive and full of vitality. It's our birthright to feel this way. Yet because of our life conditions that we discussed in the first section, so many of us have fallen off course.

But not you. You are right back on course, feeling more alive than you have in years. And other people feel this from you now too.

Those same synchronicities that you had access to on your retreat come to you clear as water in your daily life now. It's as if the pause of your retreat has opened a window to the connectedness of the world. The signs and insights were surrounding you before, but now you have the ability to decode them.

So this is what's happening in your world. This is why so many people are drawn to you. This is why suddenly you feel more like a leader than you ever have before.

Leaders know in order to guide with clarity, we must continue to forge our own clear vision. We must model it before we can share it. And retreating allows you to be the model, the leader, the creator of life, and the driver of your own ship. Your taking space for yourself will inspire others to do the same for themselves.

What you thought seemed selfish—taking time away for yourself—actually serves everyone around you. And this is the benefit of retreat. Our world needs more people who are willing to go against the normalized flow of life and say, "No! Not me, too much, slow down, I need a break, I need to fill back up." Because it is so seductive to get lost in the race.

Taking regular retreats for yourself enables you to become the sage, leader, queen, or king our world so desperately needs (and you always knew you were). Your act that seemed so small has a ripple effect for so many.

Good work.

Chapter 26

THE
NEW YOU

Every success story is a tale of constant adaptation, revision and change.
—Richard Branson, "Richard Branson's
1 Rule for Embracing Change"

Transitioning after a retreat is a not often discussed but essential piece of your experience that must be considered if you wish to keep your magnetic vibration strong.

Whatever your takeaways from your retreat are, it's important to get them squared away before you drop back into your home life. In this chapter, we'll discuss five factors to consider when transitioning back home.

- environment
- intimate relationship
- close friends
- commitments
- one deep connection

ENVIRONMENT

One of the challenges of transitioning back home is that we are all creatures of habit. And often, our environment triggers our habits, for better or for worse. So if you uncovered some of your own disempowering habits while you were away on retreat, you need to think about shifting your environment once you get home. This will better support the new version of you that you intend to carry forward.

You may need to create a space for meditation, change what's in your cupboard, or tidy up your office—it's different for every retreatant. But it is worth both thinking through and making any environmental shifts in your home or work life *within the first few days* after you return. You want your environment to set you up for success.

Below are some questions to ask yourself when thinking about your primary environments at home. Remember, if you do not create and manage your environment, it will manage you! Consider the following five elements when thinking about your home and your life.

Questions about Your Environment

1. *Space:* Do I need to update my space (living space, workspace, even refrigerator or car!)?
2. *Earth:* How does my environment support the cycles of my body (sleeping, eating, moving)? Do I need to update my space to support any new habits related to my body?
3. *Fire:* Do I feel inspired in my environment? Do I need to make any shifts to more easily access my passion and ambition?
4. *Air:* How do I manage my time? Do I schedule space for the new elements that will be a part of my life going forward? Am I too solitary or too busy?
5. *Water:* Are all aspects of my life at home and at work fluid and balanced? Are any shifts necessary to maintain flow and integrity? Is there something I could bring into my life to feel more fluid?

These prompts serve as a starting point. As you try to maintain the most benefit from your transformational experience, be sure to consider every facet of your environment.

INTIMATE RELATIONSHIP

If you're in a relationship, it's critical to honor your partner and let him or her know how much you love him or her once you return home. It is tempting to come home and go on and on about how transformational your experience was. But actions speak louder than words. He or she will see the shifts you're making in your environment, and he or she certainly feel the energetic shifts that you've made in yourself through your interactions with him or her.

A partner can respond with excitement for you. Or these notable shifts can make a partner feel jealous or insecure. Your lover may worry that he or she is no longer relevant after your experience.

Furthermore, depending on your partner's habits and sense of openness to your experience, you may be dragged down or feel unsupported once you're with your beloved again. The two of you may have created some habits that need to be rewired so you'll both benefit. The habits we keep in our homes and in our relationships are incredibly important postretreat.

If you're in a loving relationship, the best thing you can do upon your return is to go out of your way to appreciate your partner. Certainly you missed them. So this appreciation is not disingenuous. But the more you shower love on them, the more they see that you benefiting yourself by taking retreat benefits everyone, including them!

At the end of retreats I host, I give my participants who are in relationships "homework" to go home and find one way to please their partner, then report back to the group. I call it the "blow job challenge." Again, this is not relevant for every couple. But I like to keep things light and fun, so this sets the tone for the conversation of how we can bring light and love into our partner's lives and thank them for supporting our new (or old) retreating habit.

Your love can be verbal, sexual, giving of time or gifts, anything at all that would make your partner feel loved. In the long run, this pays off because once your partner sees and feels how full you are, he or she will support future retreating for you and maybe even start his or her own practice of retreat.

CLOSE FRIENDS

When you return home from your retreat, others are more drawn to you than usual, as we've discussed. It's as if people sense your fullness, and wanting some of the same for themselves, they scoot closer. People who you may have had no previous involvement with before seem to come out of the woodwork. Or maybe relationships that have already been in full force want even more of you.

All of this is wonderful. But choose whom you share your time with wisely after your retreat. Because you are vibing at a whole new level, you may want to share everything and give it all away immediately.

But please, save some for yourself. Pace yourself. Postretreat is a vulnerable time. You are still molding who and how you want this new version of yourself to be in the world. Don't give it all away before you've settled into your own new sense of being.

If you realized you need to let some unhealthy relationships go that you'd been working so hard to maintain prior to retreat, this is an incredible insight and time to take action. Go easy on yourself and let your retreat serve as the break that allows for the relationship to take its natural course. Not all friendships are meant to last a lifetime.

Be intentional about who you decide to share your time with after you get home. Remember, we are all a product of the people we spend the most time with. You must evaluate how your relationships are serving you as well as how you are serving them at every point in your life. Retreating so naturally allows for this inquiry. And now you must own it. Choose wisely. The right relationships will further bolster the benefits of your retreat.

COMMITMENTS

You've had breakthroughs and come to new understandings and ideas about yourself in your time away. Many of these came as a result of your environment of inspiration and the natural trajectory while on retreat.

But as we've discussed, it is deceivingly easy to come home and slip back into habit patterns from before that were not working so well.

Be mindful of your habits, especially the first month. Remember at least *one* commitment, idea, or shift you want to honor in yourself back home.

Maybe you decided you'd go to the gym in the morning. Maybe you committed to going on another retreat. Maybe you decided to finally end that relationship that was not fulfilling or start that project that's been brewing in you or quit that job that is sucking your soul or plan a special day with your family.

Whatever it is, bring your energy up and recommit to that decision. Take an action that will help you follow through with your agreement with yourself. Be careful not to slide too easily back into all the reasons you can't. Limiting beliefs are sneaky little buggers. So keep a close eye. Stay committed to at least one action, thought, or idea you uncovered as a result of your time away.

ONE DEEP CONNECTION

After spending time digging into what really matters in life, it feels wildly unfulfilling to come home and talk about the weather. You've just had a massive shift in your life and countless personal breakthroughs.

You owe it to yourself to relive, celebrate, and hash out your experience. Verbalizing whatever parts of your experience you're comfortable sharing will further solidify and help you embody the *New You.*

Think of a person—perhaps your intimate partner, a family member, or a close friend—with whom you can go deep. Your dear friends, family connections, or partner will do it in a heartbeat. They want to know about your experience. Give them these questions to ask you, and then ask them meaningful questions as well.

Partner Questions Postretreat

- What was something meaningful you took away from your retreat?
- What was something that challenged you while on retreat?
- What is something you plan to change/add/upgrade as a result of your time away?
- What new perspective do you have on your life as a result of leaving?
- What are you working on in yourself right now?

We spend so much of our lives connecting with people around surface topics. But we are all desperate to go deep. If you can't think of a friend, answer these questions in your own head. Go there. We all feel more alive when we connect about what really matters in life.

Using these five touchpoints will help create more intention when jumping back into your life. This will further solidify the benefits of your retreat for much longer than just the time you were away. At least until your next retreat.

Chapter 27

AN INVITATION

Who looks outside, dreams.
Who looks inside, awakes.

—Carl Jung, *Jung Letters*

As I sat in the *shala* while the group of women on my retreat listened—in resting pose, with beautiful silk eye pillows—to the final meditation before the retreat was over, I began to cry. Quietly and to myself, tears dripped down my face.

I could not believe this was my life. Looking out at the ocean, surrounded by conscious sisters, not in a million years did I dream that I would be taking regular groups through the transformational process of retreat. As I looked around the room at the women relaxing, feeling renewed, in love with each other, their lives, and most importantly themselves, I wanted to pinch myself. I felt so incredibly lucky.

I wanted to reach back in time to that desperate mother at home with three young kids wondering what was wrong with her. I wanted to tell her it would be all right. That nothing was wrong with her at all. I wanted to tell her that her loneliness and desperation were merely messages prodding her to make a move.

All she needed was more of herself. Nothing more. If she could only see forward a few years to the future, she would know that everything was as it was meant to be.

But it was her pain that led her here. And even in this renewed feeling of elation, I wouldn't take her pain away from her. Without her pain, she wouldn't have known to step away to go inside.

As the group meditation closed and the women stood to say their final goodbyes, my heart swelled with a deep sense of purpose, fulfillment, and gratitude. These were emotions that many years prior felt so far out of reach.

As I watched each woman depart the retreat center, as I do after every single retreat, I felt a combination of heartbreak and relief. Heartbreak because in our short retreat together, we'd become so intimately woven, as happens at every retreat. We'd gone so deep, witnessed magic on earth, and found our inner flames again. And now our time was over. But relief because, once again, I was alone. It was just me. Brie. As I was when I started this journey. As I was before they all came. As I was years ago at home with my children. But this time, in my solitude, I found deep inner contentment.

I was full, and I was alone. And there is no more beautiful feeling than this.

O O O

By now, you know your act of retreat is not just for yourself but for all those you love. I know it seems counterintuitive. I know there are a million reasons not to go and why now is not the best time.

But if you want to live an extraordinary life, one in which your heart, mind, spirit, and life are in sync, you have to make space for your soul. I know the world doesn't show us the way. I know our typical arc of life doesn't encourage or allow for this kind of break in the action.

But you know better. And it is essential.

Being quiet can quell the anxiety you feel. Being alone can slow the pace of your outer life so your inner one will follow suit. Meditating can show you how to calm the mind and be comfortable alone again. Journaling and dancing and reading and walking and playing can bring you back to your true, creative nature. Walking with your feet on the earth can shift your very frequency so you can bring it back and share the very best of yourself with those you love.

Retreating makes way for the highest expression of you to shine forth.

On a personal note, as I write this final chapter to you, I feel tenderhearted. Writing this book was a dream I had, a vision that came into clarity on a retreat I took. Writing this book has been a sharing of my most important tool, my best-kept secret to success, inner peace, and happiness.

Retreating makes every aspect of my life healthier. From my relationship with my husband, to my friendships, to my physical body, and more. Retreating is the highest form of self-love I know. It is only when we love ourselves that we can truly love and give to others. You deserve this kind of love too.

As I write this final chapter amid the external chaos of COVID-19 and the important racial injustice uproar of 2020, I feel a sense of conviction knowing that right now and always, what the world needs are more opportunities for inner calm. From this place, we can do and be anything. From this place, we can positively influence change in our own worlds and in the greater world.

No matter what happens externally and in the world around us, retreating offers us a clear way to calm our inner swells. All we have to do is make space for ourselves.

This is not a new message. It is age old. This book is merely a reminder. It offers some stepping-stones for you to forge your own path. It shares some clues to lead you back to what you already know.

I know that you have big dreams. I know you wish to evolve again, and again, and again. And you deserve this, Dear One. Secrets and messages are waiting for you too, just as they were and always are for me.

But you have to take a risk to find them. You have to leave what is comfortable to find what is inspiring, new, quiet, and inside. You have to make space to hear and know yourself again.

This is not a onetime act. It is a lifetime practice—to know yourself so that you may know, love, and genuinely give to others. It is through retreating that you can do just that.

Committing to regular retreat for yourself is simple, but it is not easy. It is both an art and a discipline. The heroine or hero's journey is never the easy path. It is always the courageous one. So, Dear One, the time has come. I invite you to be courageous. I invite you to your own next level. I invite you to retreat.

May this book benefit you and serve as a meaningful guide. All the best on your journey.

ACKNOWLEDGMENTS

I'd like to thank all the incredible seekers who have joined me for retreat over the years. I've learned just as much from you, if not more, than you have from me. Your wellness and evolution are absolutely what drives me.

To my regular retreat participants who always show up ready and open hearted, of whom there are too many to name. You know who you are. I am so deeply thankful for you.

To my incredible Soul Sessions clients; all my former students at MS 44, Platt Middle School, and Fairview; my yoga students at The University of Colorado; and all the professional relationships in various fields of education. Thank you.

To my insightful editor Lisa Kloskin, who let me do my thing but pushed me when I needed to be pushed. Thank you. And to the entire editorial, marketing, and publicity team at Broadleaf Books, thank you.

To my former agent, Emily Keyes, who helped put the bow on this vision.

To Allie and to Dana, who listened to me sort out my thoughts in this book regularly and have believed in me ever since the beginning. Thank you. I would not be who I am without you.

To Anne Matzke of Dawson Design for the beautiful chakra image, the website guidance, and the friendship. To Carey Albertine, for continued, priceless, professional advice and a shared sick sense of humor. To Kiana Pirouz and Lauren Daniluk for your publicity guidance, humor, and goddess connection. Thank you.

To my SIT study abroad crew, who shows up in here in stories. You are still the best group I've ever been a part of. I've never grown more in such a short period of time than when I was with each of you.

To the fearless and brave women who shared their stories with unwavering vulnerability in this book so that others may benefit. I thank you. You are incredible archetypes and inspiration for all.

To my personal mentors and teachers over the years, but especially to Christina Monson and Julie Thornton, who showed me women can do things any way we damn well please. To Mrs. Mehan, James Yaffe, and Sarah Massey-Warren, who recognized my writing ability early on and encouraged me.

To Chhoje Tulku Rinpoche, who inspired my first retreats and introduced me to Buddhism, meditation, and the inner workings of my own mind. I am endlessly thankful for you.

To my writer friends near and far, including Kristina Newman, Bri Kastner, Amanda McCracken, Lissa Cullen, Stephanie Sprenger, Pam Moore, Meg Vos, Patrick Kalenzie, Rohini Grace, Adra Benjamin, and countless more.

To my brother Conor, who dug into his librarian resources and helped me research the history of retreats. And to my brother Jeremy, who has always cheered on my creativity and perseverance.

To my parents for never asking much but always giving endlessly. For *always* watching the kids so I could work, for telling me to stick with it, for believing in me and loving on me, even when I didn't always give it back.

To my babies, who are not babies anymore: Cora Rose, Kierian, and Quinton. You are the inspiration for my wellness so that I may be the best mom you could ever ask for and so that you may have a model of inner stability and wellness. Thank you for being patient with me and letting me work when you wished we could have been at the pool or playing with snakes together.

Finally, and most importantly, to my love, my Luker. I could not have lived this dream without you. Thank you for taking time out of your own crazy schedule to be with the kids during COVID so I could focus. Thank you for always believing in me, encouraging me, being my first reader always, and being my truest companion, forever.

APPENDIX

Dear One,

I know your time matters, so I thank you for choosing to spend it reading my book. Hearing about my client's successes is among my favorite part of doing this work. I'd love to know you and how retreating has changed your life.

If you'd like to connect with me, share your success, or ask a question, please send an email to hello@briedoyle.com. I'd love to know how your life has been influenced by retreating and share in this incredible journey of profound inner transformation together.

If you're interested in joining one of my retreats and accessing more retreat resources, please check out www.briedoyle.com. Subscribe to be a part of my Insider Tribe, and you'll hear about the newest retreats first there.

I look forward to connecting with you.

Big Love,
Brie

Intentions for Retreat—a List to Generate Inspiration

- to heal after a loss, breakup, or health challenge
- to rediscover what you want in a new phase of life
- to process the next steps
- to take a break from a busy pace of life
- to reconnect with yourself after having a baby
- to make art, write, draw, dance, hike, nap, read, or journal

- to make space for your next creative inspiration
- to calm your mind
- to solidify a meditation or devotional practice
- to bring more joy into your life back home
- to uncover your true feelings about something, realign with your truth, and access your power
- to love yourself even more
- to try something new and different

OBJECTIVES FOR RETREAT

I use this list of objectives for my participants on the retreats I host. Often, I will add a new one or even take something away based on the particular theme of the retreat. But this is the core of what drives my curriculum while on retreat.

- Experience a clear elevation in energy.
- Learn new meditation and breath work strategies.
- Have at least one personal breakthrough.
- Have new ideas and inspiration for how to live your life back home.
- Walk away with a stronger connection to and understanding of your feminine self.
- Create new friendships and connections.
- Activate dopamine, oxytocin, serotonin, and endorphins regularly to elevate your state and overall mind frame.

SUGGESTED FURTHER READING

These books have all significantly impacted me and influenced work over the years. For a comprehensive list, visit my website www.briedoyle.com. For now, check these out and bring one on retreat with you!

- *The Alchemist* by Paulo Coelho
- *Anatomy of the Spirit* by Caroline Myss
- *The Art of Happiness* by the Dalai Lama

- *As a Man Thinketh* by James Allen
- *The Awakened Family* and *The Conscious Parent* by Shefali Tsabary
- *Awaken the Giant Within* by Tony Robbins
- *Becoming* by Michelle Obama
- *Being Mortal* by Atul Gawande
- *Between the World and Me* by Ta-Nehisi Coates
- *Big Magic* by Elizabeth Gilbert
- *The Book of She* by Sara Avant Stover
- *The Celestine Prophecy* by James Redfield
- *Change Your Thoughts—Change Your Life* by Wayne Dyer
- *Cutting Through Spiritual Materialism* by Chögyam Trungpa Rinpoche
- *Daring Greatly, Rising Strong, The Gifts of Imperfection,* and *Braving the Wilderness* by Brené Brown
- *Gift from the Sea* by Anne Morrow Lindbergh
- *The Happiness Advantage* by Shawn Achor
- *High Performance Habits* by Brendon Burchard
- *Irresistible* by Adam Alter
- *The Life-Changing Magic of Tidying Up* by Marie Kondo
- *Man's Search for Meaning* by Viktor Frankl
- *A Mind of Your Own* by Kelly Brogan
- *Momma Zen* by Karen Maezen Miller
- *A New Earth* and *The Power of Now Journal* by Eckhart Tolle
- *The Obstacle Is the Way* by Ryan Holiday
- *The Price of Privilege* by Madeline Levine
- *Pussy: A Reclamation* by Regena Thomashauer
- *The Queen's Code* by Alison Armstrong
- *Quiet* by Susan Cain
- *Reason for Hope* by Jane Goodall
- *Rich Dad, Poor Dad* by Robert Kyosaki
- *The Seat of the Soul* by Gary Zukav
- *The Seeker's Guide* by Elizabeth Lesser
- *The 7 Habits of Highly Effective Families (and People)* by Stephen Covey
- *The Spontaneous Fulfillment of Desire* by Deepak Chopra
- *The Subtle Art of Not Giving a Fuck* by Mark Manson

APPENDIX

- *The Surrender Experiment* by Michael Singer
- *The Untethered Soul* by Michael Singer
- *When Things Fall Apart* by Pema Chödrön
- *Wishes Fulfilled* by Wayne Dyer
- *Women, Food and God* by Geneen Roth
- *Writing Down the Bones* by Natalie Goldberg
- *You Are a Badass* by Jen Sincero
- *You Can Heal Your Life* by Louise Hay
- *Zen Mind, Beginner's Mind* by Shunryū Suzuki

NOTES

Chapter 2: This Modern Life

1 Tony Robbins, "Date with Destiny," Anthony Robbins Foundation, December 2017, Palm Beach County Convention Center, Palm Beach, FL, https://tinyurl.com/yxh7oabx.
2 Marie Ennis-O'Connor, "How Much Time Do People Spend on Social Media 2019?," Medium, August 8, 2019, https://tinyurl.com/rb74gto.
3 "Key Figures behind America's Consumer Debt," Debt.org, November 7, 2019, https://tinyurl.com/y5zgel7n.
4 "The State of the 40-Hour Work Week," Credit Loan, January 14, 2019, https://tinyurl.com/y43gshme.
5 US Department of Health and Human Services, "Adolescent Mental Health Basics," Office of Population Affairs, accessed July 15, 2020, https://tinyurl.com/y4brrxpb.
6 "Adolescent Mental Health," World Health Organization, October 23, 2019, https://tinyurl.com/y6qfsc7r.

Chapter 3: The Female Predicament

1 Alison Armstrong, *Understanding Women: Unlock the Mystery*, read by the author, PAX Programs, 2012, https://tinyurl.com/y5ozjghl.
2 Armstrong.
3 Bridget Brennan, "Top 10 Things Everyone Should Know about Women Consumers," Bloomberg, January 15, 2015, https://tinyurl.com/y4zg7e6n.

Chapter 4: Retreat, Your Style

1 *Merriam-Webster*, s.v. "retreat (n.)," accessed December 2017, https://tinyurl.com/y6ysor9p.
2 Graham Wallas, *The Art of Thought* (London: Jonathan Cape, 1926), quoted in Willis Harman and Howard Rheingold, *Higher Creativity: Liberating the*

Unconscious for Breakthrough Insights (New York: Jeremy P. Tarcher, 1984), 26–27.

3 Wallas, quoted in Harman and Rheingold, 26–27.

4 Arnie Cooper, "The Fortunes of Solitude: Susan Cain on Introverts, the 'New Group Think,' and the Problems with Brainstorming," *Fast Company*, February 2, 2012, https://tinyurl.com/y35yulm6.

5 P. E. Vernon, ed., *Creativity: Selected Readings* (New York: Penguin, 1970).

6 Rudyard Kipling, *Something of Myself* (Cambridge: Cambridge University Press, 1991).

Chapter 5: Get Your Mind Right

1 "Americans Spend 30 Billion Dollars per Year on Complementary Out-of-Pocket Health Approaches," National Center for Complementary and Integrative Health, June 22, 2016, https://tinyurl.com/y6a4hncw.

2 "Mental Health Disorder Statistics," Johns Hopkins Medicine, 2020, https://tinyurl.com/y6b6xln5.

3 Mental Health America, *The State of Mental Health in America*, 2020, https://tinyurl.com/y2bd4qsk.

4 "The Shallows: This Is Your Brain Online," interview with Nicholas Carr, June 10, 2010, in *All Things Considered*, podcast, https://tinyurl.com/y4co3zzp.

5 Claudia Dreifus, "Why We Can't Look Away from Our Screens," *New York Times*, June 3, 2017, https://tinyurl.com/znkesbt.

Chapter 7: Spiritual Health

1 Jeffery Jones, "US Church Membership Down in the Past Two Decades," Gallup, April 18, 2019, https://tinyurl.com/y5vj82fy.

2 Jamie Ducharme, "You Asked: Do Religious People Live Longer?," *Time*, Health and Longevity, February 15, 2018, https://tinyurl.com/yy9wh382.

3 Bronnie Ware, *The Top Five Regrets of the Dying* (Carlsbad, CA: Hay House, 2012), 37.

Chapter 12: The Elements of Retreat

1 Kazuaki Tanahashi and Tensho Danid Schneider, *Essential Zen* (Edison, NJ: Castle Books, 1996), 21.

2 Joe Dispenza, *Breaking the Habit of Being Yourself: How to Lose Your Mind and Create a New One* (Carlsbad, CA: Hay House, 2012).

3 Harry Carpenter, *The Genie Within* (Fallbrook, CA: Harry Carpenter, 2011).

Chapter 13: What Does (Your Name Here) Want?

1 Armstrong, *Understanding Women*.

Chapter 21: Phase 5: New Frequency

1 Regena Thomashauer, *Pussy: A Reclamation* (Carlsbad, CA: Hay House, 2016).